180 BIBLE VERSES FOR CONQUERING ANXIETY FOR TEEN GUYS

PAUL KENT

180 BIBLE VERSES FOR CONQUERING ANXIETY FOR TEEN GUYS

A DEVOTIONAL

YOU are the reason we do what we do here at Barbour Publishing. We promise that we will always use our God-given talents to produce content with you in mind—and that we will remain biblically faithful, no matter what.

Thank you for being the heart of our business.

Print ISBN 979-8-89151-251-1

Published by Barbour Publishing, Inc., 1810 Barbour Drive, Uhrichsville, Ohio 44683, www.barbourbooks.com

Our mission is to inspire the world with the life-changing message of the Bible.

Printed in China.

INTRODUCTION

Anxiety? Yeah, you've met that sneaky troublemaker who lurks around every corner and loves to make you miserable.

Now let us introduce you to the all-knowing, all-powerful, all-loving God who created you and keeps you day by day. The God who is bigger, stronger, and smarter than anything that could possibly come against you. The God who has incredible plans for you, both in this life and throughout eternity.

He didn't create you for fear. He created you to love and enjoy Him, other people, and the amazing world you live in.

You can conquer anxiety, and this book will help. It all starts with knowing God through His Word, and here you'll find 180 powerful verses to help break fear's hold on you. Read the scriptures and their accompanying devotions, talk to God in prayer, and step out in faith, allowing Him to lead you into a more positive, more confident, less anxious life.

1
TAKE GOD'S WORD FOR IT

God did not give us a spirit of fear. He gave us a spirit of power and of love and of a good mind.
2 TIMOTHY 1:7 NLV

People can mean well and still say some unhelpful things. "Snap out of it!" never snapped any guy out of his anxiety. But if your parents, teachers, or friends don't really understand what you're going through, God does—because He knows you completely.

As the omniscient (all-knowing) and omnipotent (all-powerful) God who created you, He speaks a living truth that can and will change your life. . .if you let it. Today's scripture is one of His "greatest hits" for conquering anxiety: "God did not give us a spirit of fear. He gave us a spirit of power and of love and of a good mind."

Take His word for it: God wants you to be emotionally whole. Give Him your heart and whatever time He requires, and watch the good things He'll do in your life.

2
YOU'RE NEVER ALONE

"Let me give you a new command: Love one another. In the same way I loved you, you love one another. This is how everyone will recognize that you are my disciples—when they see the love you have for each other."

JOHN 13:34–35 MSG

"Solitary confinement" makes a prison sentence even worse. Not only are you locked up in jail, you're kept away from other people.

Our anxieties can make us feel like that—that we're all alone with no hope of true companionship. But nothing could be further from the truth. If you follow Jesus, He's always with you, by the Holy Spirit He sent to live inside you. And real followers of Jesus will follow His command to "love one another," including *you*.

No matter what your emotions might say, the truth is that a Christian is never really alone. If you haven't yet asked Jesus to forgive your sins and be part of your life, why not do that right now?

3
TRUSTING GOD

But those who trust in the Eternal One will regain their strength. They will soar on wings as eagles. They will run—never winded, never weary. They will walk—never tired, never faint.

Isaiah 40:31 Voice

Wouldn't you love to rise above your anxieties? Wouldn't it be great to run so fast that your fears can't catch you?

The Bible says it's possible—and not only possible, but guaranteed. The key is trust in God.

Trust is a firm, settled belief in who God is, what He can do, and how He loves you. In any relationship, trust grows over time. And while even the best human relationships will experience bumps in the road, God's perfection means He will never ever hurt you. But you need to pursue Him by reading His Word and praying, denying yourself and serving others.

If we commit to doing these things, in time we'll find ourselves rising higher, walking farther, and running faster than we ever thought possible.

4
GIVE YOURSELF TO GOD

Trust in, lean on, rely on, and have confidence in Him at all times, you people; pour out your hearts before Him. God is a refuge for us (a fortress and a high tower).

PSALM 62:8 AMPC

Sometimes guys need the help of a trained professional to conquer their anxiety. Whether that's your case or not, one thing is absolutely essential for success—that you first give your whole self to God.

His Word is packed with commands like those in today's verse. Trust Him. Rely on Him. Have confidence in Him. . .at all times. Pour out your heart before Him. Tell yourself—over and over again—that He is your refuge, your fortress, your high tower. This is a conscious decision to contradict the anxious thoughts that creep (or explode) into your mind.

Is this easy? No—good things always take effort on our part. But here's some good news: As you commit to trusting God, He makes it easier as time goes by.

5
ZIP THAT LIP

"God will fight the battle for you.
And you? You keep your mouths shut!"
Exodus 14:14 MSG

Don't you hate that negative voice in your head? It's always saying things like "You can't do this. Why even try? It's all falling apart—and it's your fault."

Know what? God hates the negative voice in your head too. That kind of destructive self-talk doesn't come from Him. It's just another way the devil tries to keep people down. And sadly, it can be very effective.

But "the Spirit in you is far stronger than anything in the world" (1 John 4:4 MSG). The Bible is talking about *God's* Spirit, who lives inside Christians and provides the power you need to rise above your fears.

When you start hearing words of anxiety in your head, ask God's Spirit to help you zip that lip, to keep that mouth shut. Then replace those words with God's truth: "In the Spirit's power, I can do anything I need to do."

6
"THAT'S NOT MY JOB"

People cannot save themselves.
But with God, all things are possible.
MATTHEW 19:26 VOICE

Ages ago, when the internet was new, memers discovered the joy of adding funny captions to pictures. On a photo of a dead opossum in the middle of the road, sporting a freshly painted double yellow line over its flattened body, someone wrote, "Winner of the 'That's Not My Job' Award."

We laugh at the laziness that simply paints over roadkill, but there are some very good times and reasons to say, "That's not my job." Here's one: It's not your job to save yourself. You can never be good enough in your own strength to win God's approval. That is a gift of His grace that you simply accept by faith.

We add stress and anxiety to our lives when we try to do things that only God can do. Salvation is impossible with you—but with God, all things are possible. In fact, your salvation is guaranteed when you humbly follow Jesus.

7
LIGHTEN YOUR LOAD

"Are you tired? Worn out? . . . Come to me. Get away with me and you'll recover your life. I'll show you how to take a real rest. Walk with me and work with me—watch how I do it. Learn the unforced rhythms of grace. I won't lay anything heavy or ill-fitting on you. Keep company with me and you'll learn to live freely and lightly."

MATTHEW 11:28–30 MSG

Anxiety feels like having a car strapped to your back. And not some little economy model—more like one of those huge black SUVs government agents ride in. The weight never lets up, and it's crushing.

Jesus has the solution: "Come to me." Give Him your anxieties, fears, stresses, and frustrations. How? Just say, "Lord, please take this burden that's weighing me down. Carry it for me and show me how to live freely and lightly."

Keep praying that prayer, believing that He truly wants to lighten your load. Get away with Him, regularly, to recover your life.

8
TOO MUCH NOISE

My soul is quiet and waits for God alone. My hope comes from Him. He alone is my rock and the One Who saves me. He is my strong place. I will not be shaken.

Psalm 62:5–6 NLV

It's getting tougher and tougher to find a guy who isn't plugged in. Music, podcasts, video games, you name it—a constant stream of noise pours into our ears, minds, and hearts.

Noise isn't automatically bad, though you should be very careful about what you fill your mind with. But noise can be stressful. That's why David, the author of today's psalm, quieted his soul and waited patiently for God to talk. Many times, that's going to be in the "still small voice" that the prophet Elijah experienced (1 Kings 19:12 SKJV).

Our hope comes from God alone—no one and nothing else can promise lasting peace. If you want to leave anxiety behind, practice leaving the noise behind. Get quiet with God so you will not be shaken.

9
SURE AND FEARLESS

God is our shelter and our strength. When troubles seem near, God is nearer, and He's ready to help. So why run and hide? No fear, no pacing, no biting fingernails. When the earth spins out of control, we are sure and fearless. When mountains crumble and the waters run wild, we are sure and fearless.

Psalm 46:1–2 voice

Wouldn't you like to be "sure and fearless"? It's possible, but only in God's strength.

When you read the Bible, notice how often confidence, boldness, and fearlessness are connected to God's presence in a person's life. *He* is your shelter and strength. *He* is closer than any trouble, frustration, or anxiety. *He* is the one who can make you sure and fearless.

Mountains will crumble and waters will run wild, both literally and figuratively. You don't have to be anxious, but don't try to create your own confidence. Get closer to God and ask for His strength. He will respond, and your sureness—in Him—will grow.

10
MORE STUFF WON'T HELP

Don't be obsessed with getting more material things. Be relaxed with what you have. Since God assured us, "I'll never let you down, never walk off and leave you," we can boldly quote, God is there, ready to help; I'm fearless no matter what. Who or what can get to me?

HEBREWS 13:5–6 MSG

It may seem backward, but having more stuff can actually increase your stress and anxiety. Sometimes we think, "If I only had more money, better clothes, a nicer place, or (add your particular desire here), I'll feel better." But that's not necessarily true.

All physical things—and that even includes the people we care about—will ultimately go away. But if you're a Christian, God will always be with you. And having the Creator and owner of the entire universe as your adoptive Father, you truly possess everything. Then you can say, "God is there, ready to help; I'm fearless no matter what. Who or what can get to me?"

11
NEW EVERY MORNING

It is because of the Lord's mercy and loving-kindness that we are not consumed, because His [tender] compassions fail not. They are new every morning; great and abundant is Your stability and faithfulness.

LAMENTATIONS 3:22–23 AMPC

Anxiety may seem like a permanent, unchanging part of our lives. But that's not true—*God* is the only permanent, unchanging reality (Hebrews 13:8). And He's kind enough to show us new compassions every morning. The fact that you wake up with the sun in the sky, air in your lungs, and God's Spirit in your soul proves His mercy and loving-kindness.

Does that mean life will be easy? No. Jesus promised trouble in this world (John 16:33), and besides today's scripture, found right in the middle of Lamentations, that entire book is hard.

But God is entirely good. He's always present, ready to fight your battles with you. And He's prepared an incredible, anxiety-free eternity.

Because of His tender compassion, you can survive *and thrive* in this life.

12

THIS!

I pray that you will be able to understand how wide and how long and how high and how deep His love is. I pray that you will know the love of Christ. His love goes beyond anything we can understand. I pray that you will be filled with God Himself.

EPHESIANS 3:18–19 NLV

This! This is the cure for anxiety and fear.

As we come to understand God better, as we grow in the knowledge of His great love and compassion, our anxieties inevitably become less. Sure, they'll try to hang around, and they might even cause us stress from time to time—we're still human, of course, and won't be perfect until we're in God's presence in eternity.

But a growing understanding and appreciation of God will help to tame our fears and free us to live the lives He calls us to, not full of fear but of confidence, trust, and happiness in Him. This is your goal: to be filled with God Himself.

13
GETTING BEYOND OURSELVES

Then disciple them. Form them in the practices and postures that I have taught you, and show them how to follow the commands I have laid down for you. And I will be with you, day after day, to the end of the age.

MATTHEW 28:20 VOICE

Anxiety, fear, depression, hopelessness—our most difficult challenges often have a common denominator: They wall us off from other people and make us feel terribly alone.

But God made people *for* people, to engage with each other in countless positive ways. And the most important is helping others to know Jesus.

Matthew 28:20 is part of the Lord's "Great Commission," the job He assigned to all of His followers. Telling others about Jesus can be frightening, but He provides strength and courage when you try. And when someone responds by choosing to follow Christ, joy wipes out any anxiety and fear.

Showing love to others—offering them the life- and eternity-changing message of Christ—is a great way of getting beyond ourselves.

14
THE PROPER VIEW OF GOD

The L*ORD* *is merciful and compassionate,*
slow to get angry and filled with unfailing love.
PSALM 145:8 NLT

Some anxiety bubbles up from an incorrect view of God. Yes, He is holy and righteous and hates sin with a white-hot passion. *But*. . .reread today's scripture to see His attitude toward the people He created and sustains from day to day.

God loves people—so much that He would take on human flesh and die on a cross to pay the price for sin. If you have believed that truth and received the salvation that Jesus offers, God is fully on your side.

Here's the balance we all need to find: God saves us based on His love and grace. We simply accept that gift, then—by the power He provides—obey His Word. He knows we'll sometimes fail, *but*. . .reread today's scripture one more time.

As the apostle Paul put it, "If God is for us, who can ever be against us?" (Romans 8:31 NLT).

15
AFTER YOU'VE SINNED. . .

But if we own up to our sins, God shows that He is faithful and just by forgiving us of our sins and purifying us from the pollution of all the bad things we have done.

1 JOHN 1:9 VOICE

We've seen that "the LORD is merciful and compassionate, slow to get angry and filled with unfailing love" (Psalm 145:8 NLT). He knows we're all sinful people in a sinful world doing sinful things. This will continue until the day He makes us perfect in His presence.

For now, we should work hard to obey God. But when we fail—and everyone will—1 John 1:9 provides hope and peace. We simply "own up to" our sins (other Bible versions may say "confess"). The idea is that we humbly agree with God that *we* were wrong. When He sees that attitude, He's quick to forgive, to purify us "from the pollution of all the bad things we have done."

And what a stress reliever that is!

16
"LET GO AND LET GOD"?

Do not worry. Learn to pray about everything. Give thanks to God as you ask Him for what you need. The peace of God is much greater than the human mind can understand. This peace will keep your hearts and minds through Christ Jesus.

PHILIPPIANS 4:6–7 NLV

Ever heard the phrase in the title above? It's about allowing God to be God, doing the things that only He can. For example, only He can save your soul—don't stress over making yourself "good enough" for Him. Jesus was the only human being good enough for God, and He willingly took your punishment on the cross. All you need to do is accept His gift of salvation.

But once you're saved, God has responsibilities for *you*. Look at the commands in today's scripture: Don't worry. Learn to pray. Be thankful. These are all commitments for you to make. They take time and work—but the payoff is a peace that is more powerful than human understanding.

17

CONTENTMENT

So be content with who you are, and don't put on airs. God's strong hand is on you; he'll promote you at the right time. Live carefree before God; he is most careful with you.

1 PETER 5:6–7 MSG

God knew exactly what He was doing when He made you *you*. Often we create anxiety in our lives by wishing we were someone else—or at least wanting to change things that aren't changeable. But God tells us to be content with who we are. And anything He commands, He'll help us to do.

Talk to Him about your anxieties, fears, and disappointments. Spend time in His Word, not just reading but studying and memorizing it. Listen for what He's saying to you—God may point out some things that you can and should change. On other things, He'll remind you that you're perfectly fine the way He made you.

Do *your* job—pursuing God, honoring your parents, getting your education—and let God do His. He'll promote you at the right time.

18

THE MIND VIRUS

"I tell you this: Do not worry about your life. Do not worry about what you are going to eat and drink. Do not worry about what you are going to wear. Is not life more important than food? Is not the body more important than clothes? . . . Which of you can make himself a little taller by worrying?"

MATTHEW 6:25, 27 NLV

Worry is a mind virus. Once it gets into our head, it infects everything we do and say.

While worry might seem like an inevitable part of our lives, Jesus said that's not true. His rule was simple: Don't worry.

Of course, "simple" doesn't always mean "easy." The rule is clear and understandable. The tough part is putting it into practice.

But we must. And Jesus showed why we don't have to worry—because His Father in heaven knows every need we have, and He's ready to fulfill them (Matthew 6:31–33).

Don't let that mind virus steal the peace God wants you to enjoy.

19
PERFECT PEACE

"Peace I leave with you; My [perfect] peace I give to you; not as the world gives do I give to you. Do not let your heart be troubled, nor let it be afraid. [Let My perfect peace calm you in every circumstance and give you courage and strength for every challenge.]"

JOHN 14:27 AMP

Jesus understands your anxiety. One reason He came to earth to live as a man was so He could sympathize with His human creation—to experience "exactly how it feels to be human" (Hebrews 4:15 AMP). But Jesus most certainly doesn't have the limitations we do, so He can promise a peace that overcomes our troubles and gives us courage and strength.

You were not made to live in fear. But don't allow your anxiety to layer added guilt to the stress you feel. If these troubles aren't "common to human experience" (1 Corinthians 10:13 AMP), why do you think Jesus would offer us His perfect peace?

20
BANISH THE INSULTS

You see, God did not give us a cowardly spirit but a powerful, loving, and disciplined spirit.
2 TIMOTHY 1:7 VOICE

Yes, we all deal with a certain amount of anxiety. We all have fears. But that doesn't mean we're losers, wimps, or cowards. Insulting names are never helpful.

Sadly, those names are often coming from your own head, in your own voice. This is a perfect time to tell yourself, "No!"

Banish the insults. Tell yourself—really, say it to yourself, even out loud—"I have a powerful, loving, and disciplined spirit from God Himself. I can do anything I need to do, in God's strength. I am fully loved by my perfect heavenly Father. By His goodness, I will face my responsibilities, opportunities, and fears with courage."

Take the first step of changing your self-talk. Consciously remind yourself of who you are in Christ—an adopted son of God. Do this consistently, and in time you'll find yourself developing that powerful, loving, and disciplined spirit.

21
INTIMIDATION

"Have I not commanded you? Be strong and courageous! Do not be terrified or dismayed (intimidated), for the LORD your God is with you wherever you go."

JOSHUA 1:9 AMP

There are times in life when you just feel overmatched. Maybe you're lined up against a six-foot, five-inch, 350-pound tackle. Maybe a professional musician has joined your jam session. Maybe the new guy in youth group has Hollywood good looks. Situations like this can be intimidating.

Notice the word-within-a-word there? To "intimidate" is to make "timid," lacking in courage or boldness. But God's message to Joshua is what He says to each of us: Be strong. Be courageous. Don't be dismayed or intimidated.

Why? Because you're so amazing on your own? No. . .though God did make you a uniquely gifted person for your particular time and place. But you can be fearless and brave because He is always with you.

You'll still face challenging people and situations. But with God on your side, you need not be intimidated.

22
EXPECT SUFFERING

In his kindness God called you to share in
his eternal glory by means of Christ Jesus.
So after you have suffered a little while,
he will restore, support, and strengthen you,
and he will place you on a firm foundation.
1 PETER 5:10 NLT

Nobody likes to suffer. But God's Word is honest about the suffering we'll face in this world.

Anxiety is one form of suffering. That's the bad news. But there's also good news in today's scripture: Our suffering is only for "a little while."

This fifth chapter of 1 Peter describes the trouble Satan throws at Jesus' followers. Sometimes Christians are persecuted by other people. Sometimes our challenges arise in our own minds through the whispering of Satan and his demons. But never forget what John tells us: "The Spirit who lives in you is greater than the spirit who lives in the world" (1 John 4:4 NLT).

Our struggles in this life only point us toward the perfection of the next.

23

TROUBLES ARE REAL

Pile your troubles on GOD's shoulders—he'll carry your load, he'll help you out. He'll never let good people topple into ruin. But you, God, will throw the others into a muddy bog, cut the lifespan of assassins and traitors in half.

PSALM 55:22-23 MSG

Trying to be helpful, many people will downplay your anxiety. "Oh, it's nothing," they say. "Just get up and get going."

They're half right. It's true that we can't allow our anxiety to keep us from living life. But they're wrong when they say our troubles aren't real—of course they're real. Why else would God's Word tell you to "pile your troubles on GOD's shoulders"?

Human fears are one of a million kinds of trouble, a price we pay for living in a sinful world. But for followers of Jesus, that's not the end of the story.

Yes, troubles are real. But reread the rest of today's scripture to see that the promise of God's help is just as real—and more powerful.

24

TRUSTING GOD

Trust God from the bottom of your heart;
don't try to figure out everything on your own.
Listen for God's voice in everything you do,
everywhere you go; he's the one who will keep
you on track. Don't assume that you know it all.
Proverbs 3:5–7 msg

It's easy to say but often hard to do: "I trust God."

Logically speaking, trusting God should be the norm. If He has the infinite wisdom and power to make and keep us, we as finite human beings should gladly place our full faith in Him.

But sin—which affects everyone (Romans 3:23)—breaks our trust in God. Once we come to Jesus by faith, though, the Holy Spirit will help us to trust God fully. We just need to let Him work in our lives.

How? For one thing, "don't assume that you know it all." Don't let your fears tell you things that contradict God's Word. Consciously remind yourself that God knows best—and has your best interests at heart.

25
GOD PLANS GOOD FOR YOU

"For I know the plans I have for you," says the Eternal, "plans for peace, not evil, to give you a future and hope—never forget that."
JEREMIAH 29:11 VOICE

If you want to build a house, bake a cake, or write a novel, you start with a plan. It might be a blueprint or an online recipe or just an outline in your head—but as a creator, you want your project to turn out well.

As the Creator (notice the definite article and capital *C*), God wants His work to turn out well too. And you are one of His "projects"! Like the exiles from Israel in Jeremiah's day, you are in God's mind and heart. He has plans for your peace, hope, and future.

God's infinite knowledge allows Him to develop perfect plans for everyone who chooses to follow Jesus—and God already has "contingency plans" for the times you'll stumble and need extra help.

He has great plans for you. Work with Him.

26
LIVE IN THE NOW

"Give your entire attention to what God is doing right now, and don't get worked up about what may or may not happen tomorrow. God will help you deal with whatever hard things come up when the time comes."

MATTHEW 6:34 MSG

Ever heard the phrase "Don't borrow trouble"? It's a quick summary of Jesus' words above.

Jesus said lots of incredibly wise things. You would expect that, since He's God! In His Sermon on the Mount, He taught us to live in this moment, not allowing ourselves to worry about what might happen tomorrow or next week or five years from now. As the New International Version quotes Jesus in this verse, "Each day has enough trouble of its own."

That's why we shouldn't borrow trouble from the future. And that's why Jesus' promise of His perfect, unbroken presence in our lives (Matthew 28:20) is so valuable.

Live in the now. Tomorrow's troubles may never come. Either way, you're in Jesus' care.

27
STUBBORN STINKS

The LORD says, "I will guide you along the best pathway for your life. I will advise you and watch over you. Do not be like a senseless horse or mule that needs a bit and bridle to keep it under control."

PSALM 32:8–9 NLT

Anxiety weighs us down and makes us feel weak. And yet our crazy human nature can still work up the strength to resist God and His instructions.

If you have the energy to fight, battle your own stubbornness, not God's loving guidance. He wants to show you the best path through this hard world. God has full knowledge of your needs and the generous love to meet them—as long as you're willing to work with Him.

In His power, God can handle you like a "senseless horse or mule," using a bit or bridle to lead you in His way. Why force that? Don't fight God—it only adds stress to life. Stubborn stinks. Obedience is happiness for the child of God.

28 WHY AM I SUFFERING?

Many are the sorrows of the sinful.
But loving-kindness will be all around
the man who trusts in the Lord.
PSALM 32:10 NLV

Sometimes our own sin creates the emotional struggles we face. But sometimes it doesn't. When you ask yourself why you're suffering, make sure the answer you come to is true—otherwise, you'll add unnecessary weight to your burden.

"The sinful"—people who knowingly live in sin—will face many sorrows, either in this life or in the world to come, or both. But "the man" (or teen guy) who trusts in the Lord is surrounded by God's loving-kindness. Part of trusting the Lord is recognizing His holiness and quickly confessing the daily sins we commit. When we do these things, we gain God's forgiveness, plus His peace that "is much greater than the human mind can understand" (Philippians 4:7 NLV).

There's no better way to fight anxiety than drawing closer to God and His goodness. "Why am I suffering?" It may be for this very reason.

29
NO NEED TO FEAR

"Don't panic. I'm with you. There's no need to fear for I'm your God. I'll give you strength. I'll help you. I'll hold you steady, keep a firm grip on you."

ISAIAH 41:10 MSG

Granted, the title of today's reading—which comes directly from today's scripture—is easier said than done. But God's Word is always 100 percent true, so the question becomes "How can I live this out?"

Anxiety brews in our mind, so that's where we must fight it. And Isaiah 41:10 gives us some powerful weapons. First, know that God is with you. If He is who He says He is (and He is!), you have the all-powerful, all-knowing God of creation on your side. And this God "is love" (1 John 4:8)—He wants to give you strength, help you, hold you steady, keep a firm grip on you.

Tell yourself these truths over and over again until they begin to choke out your anxiety. There is no need to fear.

30
SPEAKING KINDLY

Anxiety in a man's heart weighs it down,
but a good (encouraging) word makes it glad.
PROVERBS 12:25 AMP

Once in a while, someone's encouraging word can turn a whole day around. An unexpected compliment or word of cheer can snap us out of our anxious thoughts and make life brighter, at least for a while.

Hopefully, your family or friends or teachers or fellow church members are sharing good, encouraging words with you. But there's one person who should do that every time, everywhere: *you.*

Commit today to squelching negative self-talk. Never run yourself down. Always speak God's truth to yourself, in love (Ephesians 4:15). This doesn't mean you tell yourself that everything you do is right and good—but you are honest about your failures while emphasizing God's incredible love for you in Jesus Christ. Tell yourself that you are God's work in progress—and because He loves you, you can and should love yourself.

Speak kindly to all. . .including that guy in the mirror.

31

GOD IS ON YOUR SIDE

Who stood up for me against the wicked? Who took my side against evil workers? If God *hadn't been there for me, I never would have made it. The minute I said, "I'm slipping, I'm falling," your love,* God*, took hold and held me fast. When I was upset and beside myself, you calmed me down and cheered me up.*

Psalm 94:16–19 msg

When you accept God's offer of salvation through Jesus, you gain the most powerful ally ever. The Trinity—God the Father, God the Son, and God the Holy Spirit—takes your side in every conflict. Though He doesn't remove every challenge you face, He limits what "evil workers" can do to you. He takes hold of you and goes through your trials with you, calming you down and cheering you up.

This is what God can and will do as soon as you turn to Him. Tell Him when you're slipping and falling, then trust that He will come through—because He will.

32

WHEN YOU'RE CONFUSED

If you don't know what you're doing, pray to the Father. He loves to help. You'll get his help, and won't be condescended to when you ask for it. Ask boldly, believingly, without a second thought. People who "worry their prayers" are like wind-whipped waves. Don't think you're going to get anything from the Master that way, adrift at sea, keeping all your options open.

JAMES 1:5–8 MSG

Confusion is fuel for anxiety's fire. When you don't know what to do, fears can flare, licking at the supports of your emotional house. But it doesn't have to be that way.

You have a God who delights in sharing wisdom. He is thrilled when you approach Him asking for guidance. God knows everything, and He's more than willing to lead you along His good paths. You only need to ask in faith, believing that He'll do what He's promised.

When you're confused and anxious, this is the way. Be sure to take full advantage of this opportunity!

33
"ONLY A MAN"

All day long those who hate me have walked on me. For there are many who fight against me with pride. When I am afraid, I will trust in You. I praise the Word of God. I have put my trust in God. I will not be afraid. What can only a man do to me?

PSALM 56:2–4 NLV

Human beings are the pinnacle of God's creation. We are the only living things that fully reflect His image, with the ability to think, speak, create, and relate. And yet people are only microscopic specks compared to our Lord. That's a good reason not to let anyone else frighten you.

It's easy to worry over what people think of us, what they're saying about us, what terrible things they're going to do to us. But consider these two thoughts: First, many people aren't messing with you—they're worrying over all the same things. Second, you're in God's hands. What can "only a man" really do to you?

34
NO WORST-CASE SCENARIOS

"When you go through deep waters, I will be with you. When you go through rivers of difficulty, you will not drown. When you walk through the fire of oppression, you will not be burned up; the flames will not consume you."

ISAIAH 43:2 NLT

Anxiety and fear like to go to the extremes. If a particular girl doesn't say hello, "She hates me." If you have a pain in your side, "It's probably cancer."

It's true that bad things happen in this sinful, messed-up world. But God is always in control, and He has promised protection and blessing to His children.

Notice in today's scripture that the waters are deep, the rivers difficult, and the fires oppressive. For His good reasons, God allows trouble in our lives. But none of these troubles will ultimately destroy the follower of Jesus.

Ultimately is the key word here. Bodies will die, but the born-again spirit continues forever in the perfection of God's presence. Worst-case scenarios simply don't apply.

35
ON GOD'S AUTHORITY

I sought (inquired of) the Lord and required Him [of necessity and on the authority of His Word], and He heard me, and delivered me from all my fears.

PSALM 34:4 AMPC

Here's some encouragement: The fear-free life is lived on God's authority.

Left to ourselves, we will feel anxiety. We'll see a big, hard world full of disappointment, suffering, and loss.

But God's Word paints a different picture for Christian guys. Yes, our world is a mess, but in God's power—and on His authority—we can be calm and confident, even live with joy.

You've heard of the "fruit of the Spirit" (Galatians 5:22–23), those excellent qualities God develops in His children's lives. Joy is right near the top of the list, following only love. And as God grows His fruit in you, it begins to push out the anxiety. He does the work if you invite Him to. . .so seek Him out. God will hear and, in time, deliver you from all your fears.

36
TO-DO LIST

Let the peace of Christ keep you in tune with each other, in step with each other. None of this going off and doing your own thing. And cultivate thankfulness. Let the Word of Christ—the Message—have the run of the house. Give it plenty of room in your lives. Instruct and direct one another using good common sense. And sing, sing your hearts out to God! Let every detail in your lives—words, actions, whatever—be done in the name of the Master, Jesus, thanking God the Father every step of the way.

COLOSSIANS 3:15–17 MSG

It's important to understand how salvation and the Christian life work so we're not adding unnecessary stress to our lives.

Salvation is totally free, completely God's work by your faith in Jesus. You simply believe and receive.

Christian living, though, requires your effort. Spiritual growth ("sanctification") means you have choices to make, goals to pursue, work to do. Today's scripture lays out some clear, practical guidance. Doing these things will help diminish anxiety.

37

GOD KNOWS

"The heart is hopelessly dark and deceitful, a puzzle that no one can figure out. But I, God, search the heart and examine the mind. I get to the heart of the human. I get to the root of things. I treat them as they really are, not as they pretend to be."

JEREMIAH 17:9–10 MSG

This world can be tough to understand. So can our own emotions. When we wrestle with anxiety and fear, there's often an added layer of stress and frustration that arises from our inability to "get" our own feelings.

But God understands us completely. He goes deep, sorting out the fact from the fiction, the truth from the lies our own hearts tell us. And then, if we let Him, He patiently explains these things to us.

It's rarely a quick or easy process. But if you want to know exactly who you are and how to rise above your struggles, there's no better resource than the God who made—and deeply loves—you.

38

BUT WHAT ABOUT *THEM*?

Be still in the presence of the LORD, and wait patiently for him to act. Don't worry about evil people who prosper or fret about their wicked schemes.

PSALM 37:7 NLT

Evil people? Yep, the world's got plenty. Wicked schemes? Uh-huh. . .they're all around us. Do they frustrate and worry you? That sure seems like a reasonable response.

But God doesn't want you to get hung up here. Don't worry or fret, He says. Instead, consciously and intentionally tell yourself to calm down. Really! Be still. Be patient. These are acts of the will, not things that happen by chance.

When you quiet your heart and mind before God, He can show you that everything is still in His very capable hands. It's all under His control, so you don't need to worry.

"But what about *them*, Lord?" Look up Psalm 73 to read of a guy who fretted about the bad guys and their bad behaviors. . .and see how God calmed his spirit.

39
DON'T TROUBLE YOURSELF

Stop being angry. Turn away from fighting.
Do not trouble yourself. It leads only to wrong-doing.
For those who do wrong will be cut off. But those
who wait for the Lord will be given the earth.
PSALM 37:8–9 NLV

Anxiety may creep into our lives, or it may flash through like a missile. At times, there's little we can do besides pray through our current fear.

Other times, though, there are preventive measures we can take—and today's scripture offers great advice: "Do not trouble yourself."

Sometimes we plant the seeds of our own problems—whether that's anxiety, anger, or giving in to temptations. Instead of telling ourselves "stop" and "no," we dwell on our particular issues. Regarding fear, that often looks like worry over some assumed calamity that may never come.

By the power of God's Spirit, we have more control over our minds and emotions than we often realize. Right now, ask God to prepare you for the next challenge. Commit to not troubling yourself.

40
IF GOD SAYS SO. . .

"Be strong and courageous! Do not be afraid and do not panic before them. For the LORD your God will personally go ahead of you. He will neither fail you nor abandon you."

DEUTERONOMY 31:6 NLT

Is it possible to be strong and courageous? Can a guy really reject fear and panic? If God says so, yes. . .though it may be a long process to reach the goal.

The words above were spoken to the people of Israel as they prepared to enter the Promised Land. Powerful people already lived there, so Moses urged the Israelites to trade their anxieties for trust in God.

That's what the Lord wants for all of us, that we place full confidence in Him so we can live without—or sometimes in spite of—fear. Courage isn't simply the absence of fear, but it is the ability to move forward when things are scary.

When you take that step of faith, you'll find that God is already there. He's prepared the way for your ultimate success.

41

A VERSE TO REMEMBER

You will keep in perfect peace all who trust in you, all whose thoughts are fixed on you!

ISAIAH 26:3 NLT

Since peace is the opposite of anxiety, here is a verse to remember.

Though it's part of Isaiah's prophecy of the end times, this scripture applies beautifully to believers of all eras. There's simply no better way to engage our minds than to fix our thoughts on God.

He is bigger than any of our troubles. He is better than even our greatest pleasures. As Creator, keeper, and Redeemer, God is the source of every good thing in our lives.

When we "fix" our thoughts on Him—notice that that is an active, conscious effort on our part—we build trust and gain the benefit of "perfect peace."

Does this take time and energy? Yes. . .but so does everything in life that's truly worthwhile. If you want to conquer anxiety, isn't it worth challenging yourself to a little hard work? Never forget the reward!

42
THOUGHTS AND ACTIONS

Keep your minds thinking about whatever is true, whatever is respected, whatever is right, whatever is pure, whatever can be loved, and whatever is well thought of. If there is anything good and worth giving thanks for, think about these things. Keep on doing all the things you learned and received and heard from me. Do the things you saw me do. Then the God Who gives peace will be with you.

PHILIPPIANS 4:8–9 NLV

In this familiar passage, the apostle Paul lays out a two-pronged battle plan for achieving peace.

First, discipline your mind to think on good things. Is that easy? No. Is it possible? Absolutely! And Paul gives clear direction on the types of thoughts to allow into your mind: thoughts that are truthful, respectable, right, pure, lovable, good, and worthy.

Second, having set your thoughts on the right track, pursue good actions by following the example of godly men.

Do these things and "the God Who gives peace will be with you."

43
GOD'S COMMITMENT TO YOU

I am sure that God Who began the good work in you will keep on working in you until the day Jesus Christ comes again.

PHILIPPIANS 1:6 NLV

Some Christians create anxiety by worrying over their own salvation. Philippians 1:6 indicates that is unnecessary—because salvation is God's work in your life. He will see it through to ultimate success.

Now, this doesn't mean sons of God can live like the devil—once you follow Jesus, you're expected to honor God by obeying His Word. But He knows you'll occasionally fail, so He promises to forgive the sins you confess (1 John 1:9).

What *should* make you nervous is feeling no guilt or shame when you disobey. . .that's when you should question whether you really know the Lord or not. But if you're uncomfortable with your own sin, that's a good sign. You're agreeing with God, who wants to eliminate sin from your life—and He commits to finish the good work He started in you.

44
LOVE CONQUERS FEAR

Love will never invoke fear. Perfect love expels fear, particularly the fear of punishment. The one who fears punishment has not been completed through love.

1 JOHN 4:18 VOICE

Unbelievers should be frightened of God. His complete knowledge, His awesome power, and His burning hatred of sin are truths that create trembling, either now or later.

But *sons* should never feel that way. Once you accept God's gift of salvation through faith in Jesus Christ, you are adopted into His family. He becomes your loving, forgiving, and generous Father. Because He is perfect in every way, so is His love. And perfect love drives out all fear.

Even if God needs to correct you—and He does that for every one of His children at some time (Hebrews 12:6)—you can be sure He's just trying to make you more like Himself. He's not punishing; He's disciplining you, intending to grow you into the best man you can be.

There's nothing to fear in that.

45
WELL SUPPLIED

My God will give you everything you need because of His great riches in Christ Jesus.
PHILIPPIANS 4:19 NLV

We might read this verse and think of food, clothing, and shelter. Those are certainly human requirements that God supplies, and in the preceding verses, the apostle Paul thanked the church at Philippi for providing a money gift for his physical needs.

But the rest of the chapter deals with spiritual needs, things like faithfulness, joy, answered prayer, and peace. When Paul said, "God will give you everything you need," he meant it. You don't have to worry about anything when God promises everything.

But note that God provides for your *needs*, not necessarily every *want*. He's not obligated to drop a million bucks into your bank account or make the head cheerleader fall in love with you. But as you get to know Him better, your desires will align more perfectly with His—and you can move forward in confidence, knowing that you will always be well supplied.

46

STRUGGLING TO PRAY?

A similar thing happens when we pray. We are weak and do not know how to pray, so the Spirit steps in and articulates prayers for us with groaning too profound for words. Don't you know that He who pursues and explores the human heart intimately knows the Spirit's mind because He pleads to God for His saints to align their lives with the will of God?

ROMANS 8:26–27 VOICE

Sometimes life feels so overwhelming that we even struggle to pray. Prayer is simply talking with God, so when we can't do that, we feel an added stress emotionally.

But you know what? God has already planned for that. He's got you covered.

The Holy Spirit, the third member of the Trinity (besides God the Father and Jesus the Son), steps in to pray for you. God Himself—the member of the Trinity who lives inside Jesus' followers—prays to the Father for you. And because God is all-knowing, the Spirit's prayers are exactly what you need most.

47
"ALL THESE THINGS"

So do not consume yourselves with questions:
What will we eat? What will we drink? What will
we wear? Outsiders make themselves frantic
over such questions; they don't realize that your
heavenly Father knows exactly what you need.
Seek first the kingdom of God and His righteousness,
and then all these things will be given to you too.
MATTHEW 6:31–33 VOICE

Your mom or dad might feel more of the stress that Jesus describes in this passage—the pressure of providing food, clothing, and housing in a world of economic uncertainty.

But you might experience similar stresses. How will I pay for college? Where can I find a good job? Why do others seem to have so much more than I do?

Jesus' advice is simple: Don't worry. And it's easier to avoid that worry when you recognize the truth of God's infinite knowledge and resources. He knows "exactly what you need." And He'll give you "all these things" as you actively pursue Him and His righteousness.

48
GOD WINS

Say to those with fearful hearts, "Be strong, and do not fear, for your God is coming to destroy your enemies. He is coming to save you."

ISAIAH 35:4 NLT

Many of God's Old Testament promises were specific to the nation of Israel—but they provide a glimpse into His heart for those of us who follow Jesus today.

Just as God declared He would protect and avenge Israel, He'll ultimately do the same for Christians.

If the mockery and persecution from evil people creates anxiety in you, know that God is planning someday to sweep away everyone who troubles His much-loved children. He will give even the wicked many opportunities to turn from their ways. . .but if they persist in their sin, they will face serious consequences. As the apostle Paul put it, "In his justice he will pay back those who persecute you" (2 Thessalonians 1:6 NLT).

Whatever happens in this life, know that God will ultimately win. And you will enjoy His victory.

49
LIGHT, RESCUE, FORTRESS

The Eternal is my light amidst my darkness and my rescue in times of trouble. So whom shall I fear? He surrounds me with a fortress of protection. So nothing should cause me alarm.

PSALM 27:1 VOICE

How many ways can we describe our good, loving, and powerful God? In this first verse of Psalm 27, David uses three picturesque and encouraging terms.

First, God is light in our darkness. Times of fear and confusion melt away when God's light turns our nighttime into day.

Next, God is our rescue in times of trouble. Like a lifeguard to a drowning man or a firefighter to the person trapped in a burning building, the Lord rushes to our side to keep us from serious harm. . .or even death.

And finally, God is like a fortress, an imposing stone castle, surrounding us with solid walls that keep our enemies at bay.

"So whom shall I fear?" David asks. "Nothing should cause me [or any follower of Christ] alarm."

50
"DO NOT BE AFRAID"

But now the Lord Who made you. . .O Israel, says, "Do not be afraid. For I have bought you and made you free. I have called you by name. You are Mine!"

ISAIAH 43:1 NLV

Here is another Old Testament verse directed to the nation of Israel. But all of the reasons the Israelites were told not to fear are repeated for us as Christians in the New Testament.

God "made you" (1 Peter 4:19). He "bought you with a great price" (1 Corinthians 6:20). Jesus Christ "made us free" (Galatians 5:1). He "calls his own sheep by name" (John 10:3). And Jesus declares, "You belong to Me" (John 15:21, all quotations NLV).

For all of these reasons, a Christian guy can live unafraid. Fear will sometimes arise in your heart—but by reminding yourself of the awesome God's deep involvement in your life, you can start to leave your anxieties behind and live in the emotional freedom He offers.

51

TWO WORRIES OFF THE LIST. . .

"Do not worry about your life, what you are going to eat. Do not worry about your body, what you are going to wear. Life is worth more than food. The body is worth more than clothes."

LUKE 12:22–23 NLV

Physical things can cause us anxiety—far too much, really. Though few of us worry about literally starving or going naked, we might fret over not having the "right" clothes or food. In a word, *don't*.

If you follow Jesus, you're going to be fine. He says "do not worry" because His Father (who is your Father too) knows exactly what you need. And He will take care of you.

Over the next few verses, Jesus reminds us of the way God feeds the birds—and we are worth much more than birds to Him (Luke 12:24). And God beautifully clothes the flowers that last only a short time. He'll certainly provide the clothes you need (verse 28).

So there—take two worries off your list!

52
GOD IS BIGGER

I look up to the mountains; does my strength come from mountains? No, my strength comes from God, who made heaven, and earth, and mountains.

PSALM 121:1–2 MSG

Our anxieties might seem bigger than the mountains. Our minds whirl, our hearts race, and we can't imagine getting past that giant chunk of rock called Fear.

But the Christian guy has a resource even bigger than a mountain: the all-powerful, omnipresent God who created the mountains. Actually, He made the entire universe simply by speaking. (He didn't even break a sweat.)

This is absolute truth, and it's life changing—though perhaps not immediately. So tell yourself every day, several times a day as needed, "Does my strength come from mountains? No, my strength comes from God, who made heaven, and earth, and mountains." Remind yourself that God is bigger. . .than any mountain, any fear, any other person, thing, or idea anywhere.

Consciously commit yourself to Him, and stick with it. In time, you'll find the strength He promises.

53

GET SOME FRESH AIR

He lets me rest in green meadows; he leads me beside peaceful streams. He renews my strength. He guides me along right paths, bringing honor to his name.

PSALM 23:2–3 NLT

Psalm 23 is a favorite Bible passage for many people. Everyone, it seems, loves the idea of the Lord as a shepherd, guiding and protecting His flock.

The imagery is beautiful—fluffy sheep, green meadows, peaceful streams, right pathways. Though the psalm is making a spiritual point from common physical realities, perhaps this kind of natural setting could help to calm our anxieties.

Really. Turn off all tech, go outside, breathe the fresh air. God created nature for our pleasure and benefit. And though our world is marred by sin, it still maintains much of its beauty and power to rejuvenate.

Of course, every such benefit originates with God Himself, so keep Him top of mind as you enjoy His creation. Rest and renew, and bring honor to His name.

54

THE ULTIMATE FEAR DEFANGED

The Eternal is my shepherd, He cares for me always. . . . Even in the unending shadows of death's darkness, I am not overcome by fear. Because You are with me in those dark moments, near with Your protection and guidance, I am comforted.

PSALM 23:1, 4 VOICE

What causes the most anxiety among people? We may be afraid of snakes, public speaking, or cancer. . .but the ultimate human fear is death.

Thankfully, God has provided the antidote: "Since we, the children, are all creatures of flesh and blood, Jesus took on flesh and blood, so that by dying He could destroy the one who held power over death—the devil—and destroy the fear of death that has always held people captive" (Hebrews 2:14–15 VOICE).

That passage elaborates on Psalm 23, which says the nearness, guidance, and protection of the Lord, our shepherd, keeps the "shadows of death's darkness" at bay.

Keep walking, *through* your anxiety, knowing Jesus is at your side. He will help you.

55

BETTER DAYS ARE COMING

You serve me a six-course dinner right in front of my enemies. You revive my drooping head; my cup brims with blessing. Your beauty and love chase after me every day of my life. I'm back home in the house of GOD *for the rest of my life.*

PSALM 23:5–6 MSG

Here is the end of the much-loved twenty-third Psalm. It describes the better days ahead for God's children—the perfect happiness of eternity in the Lord's presence.

"Better days" is an accurate phrase since the previous verse in Psalm 23 describes a fearsome valley of deathly shadows. Life on this earth is often dreary, sad, and scary. If you feel anxious at times, don't be surprised or embarrassed.

But do keep moving forward, reminding yourself regularly of your strong and loving shepherd, Jesus, who goes with you through every experience.

In time, He'll bring you through the immediate challenge. . .and ultimately carry you home to heaven. Be sure that better days are coming.

56
AVOID THE TRAP

Fearing people is a dangerous trap,
but trusting the LORD means safety.
PROVERBS 29:25 NLT

Why do we fear people? We may worry that our peers will laugh at us. We may tiptoe around an irritable teacher, coach, or boss. We may be afraid of disappointing our parents. We may think criminals or terrorists are going to harm us.

To some extent, these are all legitimate concerns. Peer pressure can be positive, causing us to behave better in public. Working hard for the rightful authorities helps us to grow and mature. Avoiding truly dangerous people is wise and good.

But overemphasizing the fear of people is—as Proverbs says—a trap. And we're likely to end up there when we lose focus on the Lord.

Safety comes from "trusting" Him. But how? We have to take a breath (literally), focus our minds, and recommit ourselves to doing what God's Word tells us. Ask Him for specifics in your life, and keep asking until He answers. Then obey.

57
EYES ON YOURSELF

Martha was working hard getting the supper ready. She came to Jesus and said, "Do You see that my sister is not helping me? Tell her to help me."
LUKE 10:40 NLV

Stressing over other people's choices is a poor use of your time and energy. Consider the case of this woman named Martha.

Jesus loved three siblings in the town of Bethany—Martha, her sister Mary, and their brother Lazarus, the guy Jesus raised from the dead. The Lord sometimes stayed in their home, and Mary took the opportunity simply to enjoy His company.

For her part, Martha worked hard to make everything just right for her honored guest. But her passion to serve Jesus got in the way of simply being with Him. . .and before long she was complaining that her sister wasn't helping enough.

While Christians are called to watch out for others, that's not for criticizing and complaining. Unless you're looking to bless another person, wisdom says, "Keep your eyes on yourself."

58

THE ONE IMPORTANT THING

Jesus said to her, "Martha, Martha, you are worried and troubled about many things. Only a few things are important, even just one. Mary has chosen the good thing. It will not be taken away from her."

LUKE 10:41–42 NLV

Talk about unnecessary stress—Martha chose to bustle around, insisting on serving Jesus rather than just enjoying Him. In her busyness, Martha even turned against her sister Mary, demanding that Jesus tell her to help around the house.

Jesus kindly but firmly set Martha straight in Luke 10:41–42. Mary's choice to sit and talk with Jesus was the right one. In fact, knowing Him is the one important thing in life. Yes, we should serve Jesus, but that service should arise from our love for Him. And love grows as we know Him, more deeply and personally by the time we spend in His presence.

Martha jumbled her priorities, and it caused her grief. This world is already stressful enough—let's not add to it ourselves!

59
GUARANTEED TROUBLE

"But the time is coming—indeed it's here now—when you will be scattered, each one going his own way, leaving me alone. Yet I am not alone because the Father is with me. I have told you all this so that you may have peace in me. Here on earth you will have many trials and sorrows. But take heart, because I have overcome the world."

JOHN 16:32-33 NLT

Follow Jesus and all your troubles disappear! Um, no.

If you're a Christian, Jesus guarantees that you'll have "trials and sorrows." It's important to know and accept that truth so you're not surprised when trouble arises. Don't let the hardships of this sinful world—including the tensions and temptations within you—create additional anxiety. Jesus was very honest about what His followers would experience.

But He was also clear about the solution to the trials and sorrows. You can "take heart"—you can have confidence and hope—because Jesus has overcome the world. That's just as guaranteed as the troubles!

60
YOUR RESPONSIBILITY

He who takes refuge in the shelter of the Most High will be safe in the shadow of the Almighty. He will say to the Eternal, "My shelter, my mighty fortress, my God, I place all my trust in You."
PSALM 91:1–2 VOICE

God is certainly a refuge to His people. He is a shelter from the storms, a shade from the heat, a mighty fortress standing strong against any and every enemy. He is ready and willing to provide protection and safety to His own.

But did you catch your responsibility in the verses above? *You* need to "take refuge." *You* must place all your trust in Him.

God is always there, always available for every human need. But we need to run to Him, placing ourselves in His care.

These descriptions of God are metaphorical, of course—He's a *spiritual* shelter and fortress, and it's in our spirit that we run to Him for refuge. When you take that responsibility, He promises to protect you.

61

NEVER FEAR, NIGHT OR DAY

Do not be afraid of the terrors of the night, nor the arrow that flies in the day. Do not dread the disease that stalks in darkness, nor the disaster that strikes at midday.

PSALM 91:5–6 NLT

According to these verses, there *are* terrors in the nighttime and a disease that stalks in the darkness. There *is* a deadly arrow that flies in the daytime and a disaster that strikes when the sun is high. Yet there is no need to be afraid.

Why? Because God is sovereign. That means He's in total control. Whatever happens in your life will be exactly what He allows. So if arrows or diseases or disasters threaten to strike you down, be assured that God is using them for your good and His glory.

Humans have always struggled with the idea of death, but it is an absolute certainty. For Christians, death is simply the gateway to eternal life. And that's why fear is unnecessary, night or day.

62

PROTECTED BY ANGELS

He will tell His angels to care for you and keep you in all your ways. They will hold you up in their hands. So your foot will not hit against a stone. You will walk upon the lion and the snake. You will crush under your feet the young lion and the snake.

PSALM 91:11–13 NLV

Until God says your time on earth is up, you're invincible. So you can and should go through your days fearlessly.

Angels are amazing creatures, "spirits who work for God. . .sent out to help those who are to be saved" (Hebrews 1:14 NLV). And as long as you remain on God's "living list," the angels work overtime to protect you from trouble. They'll keep you from stubbed toes, snakebites, and worse.

Sometimes God will allow you to experience trouble—but even then, He can use His angels to moderate it. And if God decides your life is over, those angels will carry you into His presence (Luke 16:22).

63

GAINING GOD'S EAR

"When they call on me, I will answer;
I will be with them in trouble. I will rescue
and honor them. I will reward them with a
long life and give them my salvation."
PSALM 91:15–16 NLT

Here is an amazing and powerful promise from the Lord. But these verses do raise a question: Who are "they," the recipients of God's presence and protection?

For the answer, jump back one verse: "The LORD says, 'I will rescue those who love me. I will protect those who trust in my name'" (Psalm 91:14 NLT).

So the encouraging words of verses 15 and 16 are for people who really care about God. To love Him is to know Him more deeply through His Word—and to obey what that Word says. To trust in His name is to look to Him above and before any other person, thing, or idea.

These are the behaviors that open God's ears to our cries for help.

64
CRY OUT TO GOD

For the Eternal watches over the righteous,
and His ears are attuned to their prayers.
He is always listening. . . . When the upright need
help and cry to the Eternal, He hears their cries
and rescues them from all of their troubles.
When someone is hurting or brokenhearted, the
Eternal moves in close and revives him in his pain.
PSALM 34:15, 17–18 VOICE

Trouble and fear travel together. So do pain and anxiety. Where you find one, you usually discover the others.

For His own reasons, God allows trouble and pain, fear and anxiety to exist in our world. But He never leaves us to face them alone.

God is always watching over His children, always listening for their call. Whether you face physical dangers or emotional challenges, God is ready to rescue and revive. But He expects you to cry out for help.

Sure, God already knows when you're afraid, sad, or in trouble. But faith grows when *you* acknowledge your need to Him.

65

THE GOOD LIFE

Does anyone want to live a life that is long and prosperous? Then keep your tongue from speaking evil and your lips from telling lies! Turn away from evil and do good. Search for peace, and work to maintain it.

PSALM 34:12–14 NLT

While the world would say that "the good life" is about money and things and sex, the scripture above gives a good biblical definition. The good life is long and prosperous because it's filled with truth, goodness, and peace.

Lies, cheating, greed, and conflict all cause anxiety. While you can't avoid the stress other people cause, you can certainly choose not to add to it yourself.

Watch carefully what you say. Consciously avoid evil and follow after good. Be a peacemaker and a peace-keeper. This is God's prescription for the good life.

You don't earn salvation by doing these things—being saved enables you to choose this better way. As a follower of Jesus, make sure you're living with integrity. Anxiety feeds on inconsistency.

PRAISE GOD!

I will praise the LORD at all times. I will constantly speak his praises. I will boast only in the LORD; let all who are helpless take heart. Come, let us tell of the LORD's greatness; let us exalt his name together.

PSALM 34:1–3 NLT

A terrible aspect of anxiety is the way it turns our thoughts inward. We worry about ourselves. We criticize ourselves. We can't see any way to dig ourselves out of the hole we're in.

But this scripture offers a way up and out: praising God. He's totally worthy of your attention and affection. . .and if you're thinking of His greatness, if you're speaking that truth to yourself and others, then you're not worrying, criticizing, and depressing yourself. You only have so much mental and emotional bandwidth, so use it for better things.

We can't honor the Lord for purely selfish reasons, just to break anxiety's hold on our lives. . .but that sure is a nice side effect. Praise God!

67
EVERY ANXIETY GONE

"God will take away all their tears. There will be no more death or sorrow or crying or pain. All the old things have passed away."
REVELATION 21:4 NLV

For many of us, life on earth requires an ongoing battle against anxiety. We need to trust God daily to keep down the fears and struggles that living in a sinful world generates.

That is part of our Christian growth: learning to let God work in our lives through His Spirit. Ideally, over time, our trust in Him grows and our anxieties lessen.

But a day is coming when every anxiety will be completely gone. God is guiding His children toward an eternity that is perfect in every way—and that will include our mental, emotional, spiritual, and physical health. All the fears and frustrations of this life will be over, left behind in a totally forgotten past.

Be encouraged by that peaceful future as you live in an anxious present. Know that anxiety's days are numbered.

68

"THE LORD OF PEACE"

Now may the Lord of peace Himself grant you His peace at all times and in every way [that peace and spiritual well-being that comes to those who walk with Him, regardless of life's circumstances].

2 THESSALONIANS 3:16 AMP

Scripture contains hundreds of names and titles for God. That makes sense, since He is infinite. All those descriptions in His Word help us, as limited human beings, to better understand God.

And this name—"the Lord of peace"—is a fantastic antidote to the anxiety that often troubles our souls. Though God is at war with Satan and sin, His nature is peace. Jesus, the second member of the Trinity, died on the cross to make peace possible between human beings and God the Father (Colossians 1:19–20). According to the scripture above, this Lord of peace wants to "grant you His peace at all times and in every way."

Reread the words in brackets to see exactly how you obtain that all-encompassing peace.

69

WHO I REALLY AM

Investigate my life, O God, find out everything about me; cross-examine and test me, get a clear picture of what I'm about; see for yourself whether I've done anything wrong—then guide me on the road to eternal life.

PSALM 139:23–24 MSG

How would you feel offering this invitation to God? David basically said, "Look deep inside me, Lord. Find out everything I've done wrong." Seems like that would only add to our anxieties.

But it's actually a great way to rise above our failures and fears. God already knows all our wrong thoughts, words, and behaviors. So when we invite Him to "investigate" our lives, we're asking to be part of the cleansing process. He'll point out our sins, and we can confess and forsake them. Then, like David, we can ask God to guide us on the road to eternal life.

Let's be honest about who we really are. That's the only way to obtain God's forgiveness and grace. . .and to leave anxiety behind.

70
GOD IS ALWAYS THERE

Where can I go from Your Spirit? Or where can I run away from where You are? If I go up to heaven, You are there! If I make my bed in the place of the dead, You are there! If I take the wings of the morning or live in the farthest part of the sea, even there Your hand will lead me and Your right hand will hold me.

PSALM 139:7–10 NLV

This passage describes God's omnipresence, what we might call His "everywhereness." You can't find a corner of the universe that God's presence does not fill.

Not everyone likes that idea. Sinful people would rather not deal with an omnipresent God. Often, they try to tell themselves that He doesn't really exist.

But He does exist as the ultimate reality. And that's great news for those of us who love God and follow His Son, Jesus Christ.

Since He's always there, we're never alone. We are never beyond His love and help.

71
YOU ARE NEVER FORGOTTEN

Your thoughts are of great worth to me,
O God. How many there are! If I could number
them, there would be more than the sand.
PSALM 139:17–18 NLV

Few things are worse than feeling alone, unloved, forgotten. But as God's child, you need never suffer that pain.

If you have accepted salvation through faith in Jesus, you have taken up permanent residence in God's family—and in His mind. His thoughts toward you outnumber the grains of sand on earth!

To say that another person's thoughts toward you were that numerous would be an obvious exaggeration. Your parents and your best friend care a lot about you, but they are finite human beings.

The infinite God, though. . .now that's another story. His mind is without limit, so vast that He can (and does) think thoughts of you that outnumber the sand.

And it's not just the quantity of those thoughts; it's the quality. What God thinks of you is "of great worth." You're never forgotten.

72
BE STILL!

"Be still, and know that I am God! I will be honored by every nation. I will be honored throughout the world."
Psalm 46:10 NLT

Some Bible verses speak to multiple audiences. Psalm 46:10, following the words of verses 6 through 9, addresses the nations of earth, the people who fight each other and fight against God. The Lord commands them, like Jesus commanded a storm on the Sea of Galilee, to "Be still!" (Mark 4:39). Everything God created—all of nature and every human being—will one day honor Him as He deserves.

But Psalm 46:10 also speaks to those of us who seek to know and honor God today, since the following verse reads, "The Lord of Heaven's Armies is here among us; the God of Israel is our fortress" (Psalm 46:11 NLT). In a world of anger, stress, and anxiety, we are wise when we quiet ourselves and consciously remind our souls that we serve a powerful God who will be honored.

73

REGAIN YOUR STRENGTH

But those who trust in the Eternal One will regain their strength. They will soar on wings as eagles. They will run—never winded, never weary. They will walk—never tired, never faint.

Isaiah 40:31 voice

Anxiety and fear waste our strength. They burn energy on worries, what-ifs, and worst-case scenarios—energy we could devote to better pursuits.

It's not easy to pull our minds away from the black hole that threatens to suck us in permanently. But it is possible in God's power.

When you're stressed, shoot up a prayer, asking God to help you trust Him. Then pray another, and another, until you begin to feel His presence. Tell Him (and yourself) that you're *committing* to trust in God, even if you don't feel it at that moment.

This takes mental and emotional energy, but God will help you wrestle it back from your anxiety and fear. And in time you'll begin to regain your strength. In the long run, you'll even soar like an eagle.

74
COUNT YOUR BLESSINGS

A glad heart is good medicine,
but a broken spirit dries up the bones.
PROVERBS 17:22 NLV

It may be clichéd, but clichés stick around because there's truth to them. When you're feeling sad or stressed, count your blessings to change your mindset.

Even in our dark moments, there is good in our lives—starting with God Himself. He's given you salvation and eternal life through faith in Jesus. You're alive, residing in a remarkable creation with people who care about you. You have the necessities of food, clothing, and shelter, and—in many cases—some extra luxuries to enjoy. The list can truly go on and on.

Will this exercise break your blues immediately? Maybe, though probably not. But if you count your blessings consistently—if you commit to doing that whenever you feel the strain of anxiety, sadness, or depression building—things will ultimately change. You'll discover the medicine for your bone-drying broken spirit that leads to a glad, healthy heart.

75

THE BENEFITS OF TROUBLE

Dear brothers and sisters, when troubles of any kind come your way, consider it an opportunity for great joy. For you know that when your faith is tested, your endurance has a chance to grow. So let it grow, for when your endurance is fully developed, you will be perfect and complete, needing nothing.

JAMES 1:2–4 NLT

Who wants to be anxious, stressed, or depressed? What good can possibly come of that?

According to God, "Plenty."

In this life, everyone faces trouble. Yours may be anxiety. His may be poverty. Hers may be cancer. But every Christian's challenge is an opportunity to grow and mature in spirit.

The Bible writer James says God allows our faith to be tested so that our endurance can grow. That means that when things get tough, you stay the course. You gut it out. It's hard, and it's not much fun. But know this: Your situation will ultimately improve, either on this earth or in heaven to come.

76
"AT THE RIGHT TIME"

Happy is the person who can hold up under the trials of life. At the right time, he'll know God's sweet approval and will be crowned with life. As God has promised, the crown awaits all who love Him.

JAMES 1:12 VOICE

Several important truths appear in this verse, but let's highlight the phrase "at the right time."

Because God is all-knowing, He decides exactly the right time for you to gain victory over your struggle. You may think He's moving too slowly, that the resolution to your problem is late. But God knows best. He has the perfect timetable for you. In fact, He has such a schedule for all eight billion people on earth—and because He's God, that doesn't stretch Him a bit.

You'll reduce your anxiety by allowing God to be God. Don't try to control Him or your situation. Just do what His Word tells you and pray for His strength to "hold up." At the right time, you'll find freedom.

77
DON'T WORRY?

Here is the bottom line: do not worry about your life. Don't worry about what you will eat or what you will drink. Don't worry about how you clothe your body. Living is about more than merely eating, and the body is about more than dressing up.

MATTHEW 6:25 VOICE

Has anyone ever told you, "Don't worry"? Did that help you to stop worrying?

Chances are, "Don't worry" has a similar effect to phrases like "Calm down" and "Cheer up." They accomplish little besides making you mad.

And yet. . .in the verse above, it's Jesus Himself saying, "Don't worry." If it's coming from His mouth, the phrase must have meaning and power. We should take it to heart and not be angry.

"Don't worry" is an imperative, something that *you* need to do. Nobody else can obey that command for you. You can think it's unfair, but that doesn't change what Jesus said. Wouldn't it be better just to ask Him for the strength to not worry?

78
THE WHY OF "DON'T WORRY"

Look at the birds in the sky. They do not store food for winter. They don't plant gardens. They do not sow or reap—and yet, they are always fed because your heavenly Father feeds them. And you are even more precious to Him than a beautiful bird. If He looks after them, of course He will look after you.

MATTHEW 6:26 VOICE

At a certain age, most of us grow to hate "Because I said so!" as a reason for rules. Our minds want a logical explanation for what we've been told to do.

Well, here's the logical reason for Jesus' "Don't worry" command in Matthew 6:25. Birds don't prepare food for themselves, yet they always have enough to eat. Why? Because God provides for them.

God loves the birds He created, but He loves people—whom He made in His own image—far more. And if He provides for those birds, "of course He will look after you."

There is the why of "Don't worry."

79
EMOTIONS VERSUS LOGIC

"Can all your worries add a single moment to your life?"

MATTHEW 6:27 NLT

Emotions are a gift from God, but they can get out of hand. A certain amount of worry or fear can protect us from danger—too much leaves us paralyzed.

Logic too is a double-edged sword. When overdone, it can squeeze the feeling out of life. But logic may also tamp down the excesses of emotion. That's what Jesus was saying in Matthew 6:27.

Worry happens. It's a natural part of living in a fallen world. But it doesn't help anything. Jesus looked at worry through the lens of logic and found it lacking. While worry presents itself as a protector, Jesus said it doesn't extend your life by a moment. Some might argue that worry actually shortens your life—whether or not that's true, it certainly diminishes your quality of living.

Changing worry into logic is tough. But Jesus tells us it's possible. . .and don't forget that He once changed water into wine.

80
"CERTAINLY"

"Why worry about your clothing? Look at the lilies of the field and how they grow. They don't work or make their clothing, yet Solomon in all his glory was not dressed as beautifully as they are. And if God cares so wonderfully for wildflowers that are here today and thrown into the fire tomorrow, he will certainly care for you. Why do you have so little faith?"

MATTHEW 6:28–30 NLT

When Jesus told us not to worry, He attached an exclamation point. Well, not literally. . .but His use of the word *certainly* greatly emphasized His main point: God the Father will take care of us.

In His Sermon on the Mount, Jesus told the twelve disciples and a crowd of onlookers that it's unnecessary to fret over daily needs like clothing. Perhaps He pointed to a field of wildflowers before speaking the words of the scripture above.

Notice the emphasis: If God clothes those fragile, short-lived flowers, He will *certainly*—absolutely, undoubtedly, without question—take care of you.

81
HOW GOD WORKS

"What I'm trying to do here is to get you to relax, to not be so preoccupied with getting, so you can respond to God's giving. People who don't know God and the way he works fuss over these things, but you know both God and how he works. Steep your life in God-reality, God-initiative, God-provisions. Don't worry about missing out. You'll find all your everyday human concerns will be met."

MATTHEW 6:31–33 MSG

All through scripture, we see God providing for people. He sends sunshine and rain for everyone, even those who hate Him (Matthew 5:45). But He takes special care of followers of Jesus, who "seek first his kingdom and his righteousness" (Matthew 6:33 NIV).

God always meets needs. Wants, though, are a different thing. He's not obligated to give you a million dollars, an immediate healing, or a certain girl. He'll provide what's exactly right for you at exactly the right time.

Don't worry. You'll be covered. That's how God works.

82
PUT YOUR TRUST IN JESUS

"Do not let your heart be troubled. You have put your trust in God, put your trust in Me also."
JOHN 14:1 NLV

Belief in God is good. The Bible says that anyone who says there is no God is a fool (Psalm 14:1; 53:1). But just believing that God exists isn't enough. Scripture also says that the demons believe in God (James 2:19)! That doesn't mean demons are saved.

To be born again, to enjoy all the benefits of a real relationship with God, you have to believe in the life and work of Jesus Christ. This saving faith is what unlocks God's blessing in your life. It washes away your sins and protects you from the punishment of hell. It guarantees you a perfect eternity, as well as God's help in this life. Once you're adopted into God's family, He becomes your loving Father who will wisely and generously provide the help you need for every challenge you face.

83

NOTHING IS IMPOSSIBLE

For with God nothing is ever impossible and no word from God shall be without power or impossible of fulfillment.

LUKE 1:37 AMPC

The headline above is absolutely true and yet potentially misleading. "Nothing is impossible". . . *with God.*

If we tell ourselves "nothing is impossible" but think that's true in our own power, we'll be disappointed and stressed. False beliefs can increase anxiety, because they don't lead to good results.

But when we acknowledge God as the author of all possibilities, things change. With Him, "nothing is ever impossible." Every word He's spoken will be fulfilled.

That means it is possible to live without fear. Peace and joy are guaranteed. You will be completely happy and whole.

Keep in mind that some of these promises—like the return of Christ—may take time to be fully realized. But God's Word is certain, and better days are coming. With God, nothing will ever be impossible.

84
JOSHUA'S COMMAND AND POWER

Have not I commanded you? Be strong, vigorous, and very courageous. Be not afraid, neither be dismayed, for the Lord your God is with you wherever you go.
JOSHUA 1:9 AMPC

Don't you love scripture's honesty? Joshua was truly a heroic leader, but early in his story we learn that he felt fear and dismay. It's easy to imagine why: Joshua became the leader of Israel after the death of Moses, the larger-than-life character who faced down Pharaoh, parted the Red Sea, met God on Mount Sinai, and put up with hundreds of thousands—perhaps millions—of cranky people wandering through the desert. Now Joshua was in charge, tasked with taking these people into their promised land of Canaan. But there were powerful people already there who had no intention of giving up their property to the newcomers.

So God commanded Joshua, "Be strong, be courageous. Don't be afraid or dismayed." These commands required a superhuman power, but "the Lord your God is with you wherever you go."

85

WORRY VERSUS WORK

Which one of you can add a single hour to your life or 18 inches to your height by worrying really hard?

LUKE 12:25 VOICE

We've read similar words in Matthew 6:27. There, Jesus said, "Worrying does not do any good; who here can claim to add even an hour to his life by worrying?" (VOICE).

Luke goes further. Not only does worrying fail to add time to your life, but it comes up short (pun intended) for increasing your height. Though Jesus didn't say it, we can imagine Him teaching that worry won't add money to your bank account, A's to your report card, or a girlfriend to your side. So why worry?

Turn that nervous energy toward better things. First, to Bible study and prayer—they'll guide you into God's paths. Next, to hard work in whatever way He directs. You can't guarantee longer life or a taller body. . .but hard work will help with the bank account, grades, and maybe even the girl.

86
LIKE A TREE

But blessed is the one who trusts in Me alone; the Eternal will be his confidence. He is like a tree planted by water, sending out its roots beside the stream. It does not fear the heat or even drought. Its leaves stay green and its fruit is dependable, no matter what it faces.

JEREMIAH 17:7–8 VOICE

Wouldn't it be nice to be like a tree—from an emotional standpoint, at least? It's rooted and strong, flexible and resilient.

That's the picture God paints of the person who "trusts in Me alone." When God is our "confidence"—not our own wisdom, or goodness, or money, or any other thing we're tempted to trust in—we will be like a healthy tree. Its roots reach the nearby stream, drawing life-giving water. It stays green and produces fruit even when the rain doesn't fall and the sun beats down on it.

We can enjoy that kind of health and strength too. It starts with trusting God fully.

87
OUT OF CONTROL

The minute I said, "I'm slipping, I'm falling,"
your love, God, took hold and held me fast.
When I was upset and beside myself,
you calmed me down and cheered me up.
Psalm 94:18–19 MSG

Emotions can really mess us up. Anxieties and fears can get out of control. . .then we find *we're* out of control. Like the psalmist said, "upset and beside [ourselves]."

God has the desire and power to turn us around, putting us back on the path of calm. But did you notice what the psalmist did first? He had to honestly acknowledge his problem to God.

"Who needs a doctor: the healthy or the sick?" Jesus once asked. "I'm here inviting the sin-sick, not the spiritually-fit" (Mark 2:17 MSG). He was discussing salvation—saying people need to admit their sin before God will save them—but the principle applies to all of life. God wants us to recognize how much we need Him. That's when He steps in to restore control.

88

CONSTANT PEACE

You will guard him and keep him in perfect and constant peace whose mind [both its inclination and its character] is stayed on You, because he commits himself to You, leans on You, and hopes confidently in You.

ISAIAH 26:3 AMPC

We've already described Isaiah 26:3 as a verse to remember, since its promise of peace is the ideal counterpart to our anxieties. But let's consider this scripture again from a different Bible translation, one that brings out another element of God's "perfect peace."

The Amplified Version of the Bible, quoted above, looks into the full range of meanings for words in the original languages. . .then either translates them as phrases or adds an explanation in brackets. The "perfect peace" that Isaiah 26:3 mentions gets the amplification of "constant"—that means this peace is steady, ongoing, with us for the long term.

When we stay our minds on God, committing ourselves to Him, hoping only in Him. . .our peace will be perfect and *constant*.

89

HOWEVER YOU SAY IT. . .

"I, your God, have a firm grip on you and I'm not letting go. I'm telling you, 'Don't panic. I'm right here to help you.'"

Isaiah 41:13 MSG

Do you ever wonder where the Bible comes from? (Don't worry—we'll come back to our main theme in a moment.)

Many centuries ago, God inspired dozens of men to write down His message. These original documents—called "autographs"—have never been found. But so many ancient copies agree so closely that we're confident we know exactly what God said. Today, linguists translate the ancient text into the Bibles we read in our own languages. Other Bibles are *paraphrases*—not exact translations, but versions that use compelling language to enhance our understanding and enjoyment.

The Message, quoted above, is a paraphrase, describing God's "firm grip" on us as a reason not to "panic." Read this verse in any other translation, and you'll see the same ideas, even if in milder words. But however you say it, it's truth to live by.

90
CHRISTIANS WIN

"Count on it: Everyone who had it in for you will end up out in the cold—real losers. Those who worked against you will end up empty-handed—nothing to show for their lives. When you go out looking for your old adversaries you won't find them—not a trace of your old enemies, not even a memory."

ISAIAH 41:11-12 MSG

In this world, it doesn't look like Christians win. Selfish, dishonest, abusive people seem to get ahead, while faithful followers of Jesus are belittled, pushed aside, even tortured and killed in countries around the globe.

But never forget that this world is barely a punctuation mark in the whole book of history. If eternity goes on forever—and that's the very definition of *eternity*—the seventy or eighty years we'll live in this broken world are simply a blip. And your enemies, the people who hate you because they hated Jesus first, will be the "real losers."

No matter how tough this world becomes for Christians, in the end we'll win.

91

LESSONS FROM FARMING

So let's not allow ourselves to get fatigued doing good. At the right time we will harvest a good crop if we don't give up, or quit. Right now, therefore, every time we get the chance, let us work for the benefit of all, starting with the people closest to us in the community of faith.

GALATIANS 6:9–10 MSG

Farming? What does that have to do with anxiety?

Well, think how agriculture works. When a farmer plants seeds, he knows three things: First, whatever he plants will be the crop he reaps. Second, it's going to take time for that crop to grow and develop. Finally, he'll get back far more than the seeds he put into the ground.

Now apply these ideas to your battle with anxiety. If you consistently do good, not allowing yourself to get tired and quit, you will receive good in return. The process may take a while, but if you stay faithful, you can expect much more than you put in.

92
"A MILLION DETAILS"

Oh Martha, Martha, you are so anxious and concerned about a million details, but really, only one thing matters. Mary has chosen that one thing, and I won't take it away from her.

LUKE 10:41–42 VOICE

Do you remember meeting Martha and her sister Mary earlier in this book? They, along with their brother Lazarus, were good friends of Jesus. The Lord would sometimes visit their home for meals and fellowship.

We've seen how Mary simply sat with Jesus, enjoying His company—while Martha worked and worried over "a million details," as the Bible version called The Voice describes things. What a great phrase for what happens in anxious minds. A million (or more) details swirl around, often paralyzing our thought process. That keeps us from pursuing the more important things. . .or, in Jesus' view, the *most* important thing: Him.

Notice how Jesus commended Mary. He said she had "chosen" the one thing that truly matters. This is a choice we can and must make too.

93

NINE POWERFUL WORDS

When I am afraid, I will trust in You.
PSALM 56:3 NLV

Safety forces use very concise language to communicate important information fast. A police dispatcher will declare, "Code 10-31, at 539 Main Street," rather than saying, "Well, there's this scary-looking guy sneaking around the convenience store on Main—you know, the one with the big yellow sign—and it seems like he might just be committing a crime of some sort!"

Psalm 56:3 is an example of very concise information for addressing your moments of crisis. These nine powerful words apply to every situation that makes you anxious, and you can "dispatch" them to God in about two seconds.

"When I am afraid"—of other people, of health problems, of the future, of life in general—"I will trust in You." And why not? God's always there, always listening, always ready to steady the hearts and minds of His kids. . .those adopted sons who acknowledge their absolute need of Him.

94

CONTINUED DIFFICULTIES

"In this godless world you will continue to experience difficulties. But take heart! I've conquered the world."

JOHN 16:33 MSG

False expectations create disappointment—and often anxiety. When we assume things will go one way but they turn out the opposite, we're frustrated, angry, confused. None of those feelings help us to live in victory.

So Jesus clarifies our expectations. When you choose to follow Him, you aren't carried to heaven on flowery beds of ease, as an old hymn makes plain. No—you'll be a soldier of the cross, facing the struggles that warriors on battlefields do. In Jesus' words, you will "continue to experience difficulties." The challenges won't fully end until eternity.

We say "fully end" because God, in His kindness, often gives relief from our trials in this world. But expect them to return, again and again, until you're safe in God's presence in heaven. That will happen someday, and it's why you can "take heart." By His death and resurrection, Jesus has conquered this world.

95
DOUBLY PROTECTED

Even when I walk through the darkest valley,
I will not be afraid, for you are close beside me.
Your rod and your staff protect and comfort me.
PSALM 23:4 NLT

Psalm 23 is one of the most familiar of all Bible passages. But sometimes our familiarity with a scripture can cause us to overlook important details. For instance, the rod and the staff of verse 4.

The Lord, our shepherd, is equipped to protect and comfort us, His beloved sheep. He carries not one but two important tools for our benefit.

The staff is His walking stick, but its curved end is useful for pulling wandering sheep back from trouble. The rod is His weapon, used for punishing any predators that might try to harm us.

We travel through a dangerous world, through dark valleys that threaten us with death. But we need not fear, since the Lord is close by. And His rod and staff will always provide both protection and comfort.

96
THE GOD OF YOUR HOPE

May the God of your hope so fill you with all joy and peace in believing [through the experience of your faith] that by the power of the Holy Spirit you may abound and be overflowing (bubbling over) with hope.

ROMANS 15:13 AMPC

In times of anxiety, hope is crucial. As a follower of Jesus, you always have hope. In fact, God Himself is your hope.

Hope allows us to look past our current hardships. Hope shows us a better future. Hope keeps us moving forward.

When you recognize God as your hope, He can fill you with "all joy and peace in believing"—that is, believing in Him as your hope! He can unleash His Spirit's power in your life so you can "abound" and even overflow with hope.

No matter how hard things may be now, God has (and *is*) hope for you. He will provide the peace and joy you long for. He does these things in response to your faithful prayers.

97
FAITH

The fundamental fact of existence is that this trust in God, this faith, is the firm foundation under everything that makes life worth living. It's our handle on what we can't see. The act of faith is what distinguished our ancestors, set them above the crowd.

HEBREWS 11:1–2 MSG

The Christian life is built on faith, "our handle on what we can't see," in the words of The Message, "the evidence of things not seen," according to the King James Version.

Though "no one has ever seen God" (John 1:18 MSG), we believe in Him by faith, seeing evidence of His power and glory in creation, reading His self-description in His Word. Though we've never seen or touched Jesus, we believe by faith what the Bible says of His life and teaching, His death and resurrection.

And we take the Bible's promises of healing by faith. We believe in a God we haven't seen. So let's accept—by the same faith—the truth that He will ultimately make us whole.

98

GOD IS ON YOUR SIDE

So what should we say about all of this? If God is on our side, then tell me: whom should we fear?

ROMANS 8:31 VOICE

As the story goes, an adviser told Abraham Lincoln, president during the American Civil War, that he was glad God was on their side. Lincoln's response: "My concern is not whether God is on our side; my greatest concern is to be on God's side."

Whether Lincoln actually spoke those words or not, they carry a certain amount of truth. Our highest goal should always be to put ourselves within God's will, not try to coerce Him into performing ours.

And yet, according to the apostle Paul, God *is* on the side of everyone who follows Jesus by humble faith. When you believe in His death on the cross as payment for your sins—and His resurrection, proving His ultimate power—you are adopted into God's family forever. And He is forever on your side.

So what is there to fear?

99

LOOSE LIPS. . .

Don't let even one rotten word seep out of your mouths. Instead, offer only fresh words that build others up when they need it most. That way your good words will communicate grace to those who hear them.

EPHESIANS 4:29 VOICE

Have you ever heard the saying "Loose lips sink ships"? It dates back to World War II, when the United States government used the words as a warning. People who had information on cargo ships and warships should not speak carelessly about their comings and goings. Otherwise, the enemy could use such information to sink the vessels.

We as Christians are also wise to guard our lips. . .not to protect ships at sea but to honor the people around us. Rotten words—angry, judgmental, gossipy, hateful words—can sink another person as effectively as a torpedo does a ship.

That's a tragedy we don't want to be part of. Why not? First, because we should be concerned for other people. Second, because the guilt we'd feel would only compound our own anxieties.

100
WHAT GOD CAN DO

We know that God makes all things work together for the good of those who love Him and are chosen to be a part of His plan.
ROMANS 8:28 NLV

In a Bible full of remarkable promises, this one ranks right near the top. God, by His infinite wisdom and power, can use every circumstance of our lives to bring about good results.

So even our anxieties can work toward our good. Even our greatest disappointments and losses. Even our confusion, frustration, and depression.

Not that these things are all good by themselves. But if they point our hearts toward God, He can miraculously turn them—along with our victories—into "good," something that benefits us and honors Him.

Two requirements of Romans 8:28 are that we love God and that we were chosen to be part of His plan. If you've accepted Christ, you qualify for the second—and are capable of the first. When you consider all God can do, why wouldn't you love Him?

101

ONE-HANDED

When I walk into the thick of trouble, keep me alive in the angry turmoil. With one hand strike my foes, with your other hand save me. Finish what you started in me, GOD. Your love is eternal—don't quit on me now.

PSALM 138:7–8 MSG

Can you do a one-handed push-up? A one-handed pull-up? They're considerably harder than the two-handed variety.

That simple truth makes the imagery of Psalm 138:7–8 especially compelling. With just one hand, God can fight off all your enemies. With His other hand, He can pull you up and out of a dangerous place. Neither task wearies or weakens Him at all.

Of course, since God is a spirit, His "hands" are figurative. But that doesn't diminish the promise of His protection one bit. God fills the entire universe, and He's in control of everything, whether spiritual or physical. If He says He can manage your challenges one-handed, He absolutely can. And you can simply wait for Him to rescue you with His other hand.

102

WEAK TO STRONG

I receive joy when I am weak. I receive joy when people talk against me and make it hard for me and try to hurt me and make trouble for me. I receive joy when all these things come to me because of Christ. For when I am weak, then I am strong.

2 Corinthians 12:10 NLV

Here is a paradox of Christian living: "When I am weak, then I am strong."

What does that mean? Simply that God displays His immense power through us when we get out of the way. If we can put off our pride and admit we're weak, God will show His strength in us. But if we say, "I can do it myself," and try to solve our own problems, He'll step back and let us try. Then, after we inevitably fail, He'll give us another chance to humbly request His help.

So the apostle Paul said that weakness brought him joy, for that was when God could truly move in Paul's life.

103
SPECIFIC, BUT GENERAL

And He will be leading you. He'll be with you, and He'll never fail you or abandon you. So don't be afraid!
DEUTERONOMY 31:8 VOICE

Moses spoke the words of Deuteronomy 31:8 to his successor, Joshua. The Bible portrays the young warrior as an excellent leader, but it also records several times that he was told, "Don't be afraid." Though this encouragement was specific to Joshua, it also applies generally to all of us who follow God through faith in Jesus.

Earlier in Deuteronomy 31, Moses had told all the people of Israel that God would be with them as they crossed the Jordan River to enter the Promised Land. Just as he had said to Joshua, Moses told the people, "He'll never fail you or abandon you!" (verse 6 VOICE).

Today, God is just as committed to His children—to followers of Jesus—to *you*. He'll be with you, and He'll never fail you or abandon you. So don't be afraid!

104

ALL YOU NEED

God will generously provide all you need.
Then you will always have everything you need
and plenty left over to share with others.
2 CORINTHIANS 9:8 NLT

When the apostle Paul wrote the letters that became books in our Bible, physical needs were more pressing than today. People suffered real hunger. Medical care was primitive compared to ours. Clothing, shelter, and other necessities were more difficult to obtain. So the promise Paul made in 2 Corinthians 9:8 was very encouraging to his readers.

In the modern West, physical needs are generally less of a stress to us. But stress is still everywhere. We face anxieties and fears, pressures of all sorts from inside and outside ourselves. Still, the promise of God's provision remains.

As a generous Father, He is eager to bless you physically, spiritually, and emotionally. He provides everything you need, even if it is not always what you want. And you'll be so well supplied that He'll expect you to share the goodness with others.

105
WHAT WOULDN'T GOD GIVE YOU?

"This is how God loved the world: He gave his one and only Son, so that everyone who believes in him will not perish but have eternal life. God sent his Son into the world not to judge the world, but to save the world through him."

JOHN 3:16–17 NLT

For good reason, John 3:16 is one of the Bible's best-known verses. Christians love the truth that God sent His own Son, Jesus, to die on the cross for their sins. Even many unbelievers find the message of this verse compelling.

Jesus' life, death, and resurrection are evidence of God the Father's love for all people—anyone who accepts this "good news" by faith receives eternal life. If you've been saved, ask yourself this: Knowing that God gave His only Son for your well-being, what *wouldn't* He give you? Anything you need to be healthy and whole is something He will provide.

If you haven't yet accepted God's gift of salvation, why not now?

106
YOU'RE NOT ALONE

Energize the limp hands, strengthen the rubbery knees. Tell fearful souls, "Courage! Take heart! God is here, right here, on his way to put things right and redress all wrongs. He's on his way! He'll save you!"

Isaiah 35:3–4 MSG

You're not alone—that's a phrase with two meanings.

Meaning number one: You're not the only guy battling anxiety. Read the Bible and you'll find reference after reference to fearful people. You'll see command after command to take courage and not be afraid. Clearly, the experience of fear is common among human beings in general—even among followers of Jesus specifically.

Meaning number two: You're never alone in your struggle, since God is always with you. He is at your side, working even now toward His ultimate resolution of all things. In the words of Isaiah 35:4, God is "on his way to put things right and redress all wrongs." He's coming to save you.

And that is why you can take heart and find courage.

107

WHAT YOU NEED, WHEN YOU NEED IT

"When you are put into their hands, do not be afraid of what you are to say or how you are to say it. Whatever is given to you to say at that time, say it. It will not be you who speaks, but the Holy Spirit."

MARK 13:11 NLV

The two sets of brothers among the twelve disciples heard Jesus speak the words above. Peter and Andrew and James and John wanted to know more about Jesus' prediction of the destruction of the temple. They got an earful.

Jesus warned the four that persecution was coming. They would be taken to court and punished physically, then paraded in front of governors and kings. Their job would be to speak the truth about Jesus, no matter how frightened they might be. But it wouldn't be them speaking, actually—the Holy Spirit would provide the words they needed, just as they needed them.

That's the way God typically works in every area of our lives.

108

YOU CAN TRUST GOD

When you are tempted to do wrong, do not say, "God is tempting me." God cannot be tempted. He will never tempt anyone.

JAMES 1:13 NLV

Bad relationships add to our anxieties. If you don't trust the person you're with, you'll inevitably be uncomfortable. Happily, we don't ever need to feel that way in our relationship with God.

All human beings—even the ones we love most—have a certain level of built-in selfishness. Some are far worse than others, but everyone will occasionally mistreat us. That's just the reality of living in a sinful world.

But God, the very definition of righteousness, will always do the right thing. The temptations you face—the feelings you know are wrong but you can't seem to shake—don't come from Him. In fact, He's always eager to help you through any struggles you face.

God is a gentleman. . .He won't force His help on you. But when you turn to Him for relief, you'll receive it. You can always trust God.

109
ANGER MANAGEMENT

Understand this, my dear brothers and sisters: You must all be quick to listen, slow to speak, and slow to get angry. Human anger does not produce the righteousness God desires.

JAMES 1:19–20 NLT

"I have a quick temper" is simply a justification for angry outbursts. According to the book of James, we should (and can) be "slow to get angry."

James—probably one of Jesus' brothers (Matthew 13:55; Mark 6:3)—said Christians "must" be slow to anger. That's a command, not a suggestion.

While it may seem difficult to obey, notice that James builds up to the command with two easier rules: First, "be quick to listen," then "slow to speak." If we commit ourselves to opening our ears and shutting our mouths, our anger reaction will calm down.

With our anger increasingly under God's control, our anxiety should begin to diminish as well. We won't need to worry about embarrassing ourselves or hurting people we love. Anger management becomes a form of anxiety management.

110
GENEROUS GOD

God did not keep His own Son for Himself but gave Him for us all. Then with His Son, will He not give us all things?
ROMANS 8:32 NLV

God gets a bad rap from a lot of people—and their negativity can even begin to infect our hearts and minds as followers of Jesus.

Too many people view God as a killjoy out to keep people from having fun. Some see Him as eager to punish human beings. Others think He holds back good things out of apathy or stinginess.

None of these ideas are remotely true. The apostle Paul pointed out in Romans 8:32 that God gave up His own Son for humanity's salvation. If He was willing to do that, won't God give us any good and necessary thing?

As we've noted before, this isn't a promise of God meeting our every *desire*. But He will certainly provide for our every need in this life, and then lavish us with gifts in a perfect eternity.

111
THE STRUGGLE IS GOOD

Those who are dominated by the sinful nature think about sinful things, but those who are controlled by the Holy Spirit think about things that please the Spirit.

ROMANS 8:5 NLT

Every Christian man faces temptation. Christian women face temptation too, but we're focused on the guys here. . .and our temptations may be more physical and powerful.

Whether your particular weakness is sex or greed or anger—or, as we've been discussing, worry, fear, and anxiety—the struggle is good. If temptation bothers you, that means God's Holy Spirit is working in your life.

If you can give in to temptation without any mental debate—or feelings of guilt afterward—don't waste a moment, but ask God to save your soul.

But if temptation troubles your spirit, if you hate the internal tug-of-war you feel, cross one anxiety off your list. You are a true follower of Jesus. The struggle proves it.

Your job now is to fight your old sin nature to the death. God's Spirit will help you.

112

REWARDS AHEAD

Even if you suffer for doing what is right, God will reward you for it. So don't worry or be afraid of their threats.

1 PETER 3:14 NLT

On their list of life goals, few people would write, "Suffer!" And yet committed Christians often suffer—as residents of a broken world, as family and friends of broken people, as broken individuals predisposed to anxiety and fear. And then there's the issue of persecution, with which Satan tries to break our grip on Christ. (He overlooks the fact that it's Jesus' grip on us that matters—and nothing can break that.)

Whatever the cause of our suffering, it's hard. It's no fun. It's frustrating and frightening. But God understands that, so He inspired the apostle Peter to share the promise recorded above.

Don't let suffering get you down. Expect it. Commit to weathering every storm by the power that God Himself provides. And look ahead to the rewards of faithfulness. His perfect eternity will override every trial of this life.

113
GOD CARES FOR HIS OWN

When calamity comes, they will escape with their dignity. When famine invades the nations, they will be fed to their fill.

Psalm 37:19 voice

When David wrote Psalm 37, his nation of Israel represented God's handpicked people in the world. David had been specially chosen by God to lead them as king. The teaching and the promises of Psalm 37 had special meaning to Israel. . .but they also show us how God still cares for His own today.

As Christians—men and women, guys and girls of every age, race, and social class—we have even greater blessings than ancient Israel. They had a tabernacle (and later, a temple) where God lived in their midst. But we have God living inside us by His Holy Spirit (1 Corinthians 3:16; 6:19)!

God will certainly care for us at least as much as He did for ancient Israel. He'll see us through every calamity of this life and into His eternal presence.

114

DON'T GET DISTRACTED

"The seed cast in the weeds is the person who hears the kingdom news, but weeds of worry and illusions about getting more and wanting everything under the sun strangle what was heard, and nothing comes of it."

MATTHEW 13:22 MSG

The word *gospel* means "good news." What else would you call the message of God's gift of salvation, of the canceling of sin by simple faith in Jesus, of a perfect eternal life in God's presence? It's all free, and all yours for the asking.

That's why it's so important not to get distracted. In Matthew 13, Jesus described the gospel as seed that a farmer scattered onto different types of soil. Some people, caught up in "worry and illusions about getting more," cause the gospel to be choked out like grass among weeds.

Nothing could be better than the salvation God offers. It will help your life in every way, both now and forever. It only makes sense to be sure you've received it.

115

GOOD MEDICINE

He is ever present with me; at all times He goes before me. I will not live in fear or abandon my calling because He stands at my right hand.

PSALM 16:8 VOICE

When the Bible discusses anxiety and fear, there's a consistent theme: Because God is always with you, fear is unnecessary.

That doesn't mean fear is nonexistent. Nor does it mean that fear won't still affect us, even as committed followers of Jesus. What it means is that we must change our relationship to fear.

When fear knocks at the door of your soul, remind yourself that God is always present with you. When anxiety tries to keep you in bed or within the locked doors of your home, tell yourself, "He stands at my right hand."

These are life-changing truths, even though they may seem slow to take effect. Think of them as a medicine that counteracts a long-standing disease—you keep taking the pills until you realize you're feeling better. Stick with the program!

116

IF YOU REMEMBER JUST ONE VERSE. . .

And set your minds and keep them set on what is above (the higher things), not on the things that are on the earth.

COLOSSIANS 3:2 AMPC

. . .remember this one.

Anxiety and fear are things of this broken world. They're not in heaven and won't be in the new heavens and earth of eternity.

So while we're still here, the Bible tells us to change our focus. Yes, we're troubled human beings in a troubled world, but we know better things are coming. So we should "set" our minds on what God has promised: a kingdom where Jesus rules perfectly, tears are wiped away, sorrow and pain and death—and fear—are gone forever.

It isn't easy to set and keep our minds on "the higher things," but it's essential to our mental health. Focusing on the trials of this sinful world will only drag us down. . .and haven't we had enough of that?

If you remember just one verse from this book, remember Colossians 3:2.

117

HANG ON

"God will take away all their tears. There will be no more death or sorrow or crying or pain. All the old things have passed away."
REVELATION 21:4 NLV

Phrases like "Hang on" and "It will get better" don't seem to help in the moment, do they? And yet they carry truth that we should be willing to receive.

The Bible often urges us to be strong and steadfast—basically to "hang on" through our trials. Scripture also reminds us—often—of the incredible future God has planned for those who follow Jesus. If these are important emphases of God's Word, they are important truths for us to take hold of. Let's not become frustrated or irritated by God's own direction.

So when you're wrestling with fears and frustrations, take a step back and say, "This is temporary. No matter how stressed I am right now, God will help me through. I just need to hang on until He changes my current trouble . . .or makes everything perfect in eternity."

118

GOOD AND BAD FAKING

"Be sure you do not do good things in front of others just to be seen by them. If you do, you have no reward from your Father in heaven."

MATTHEW 6:1 NLV

If you're nervous in a social setting, some people say, "Fake it till you make it." They mean that even if you're really uncomfortable, pretend that you're enjoying yourself. After a while, you might find that you are. That's good faking.

Bad faking is when you try to convince other people of your own goodness by drawing attention to your acts of kindness and charity. Of course, you should be kind and charitable, because that reflects your Lord. But if you're looking for human approval, that's all you'll get. You won't be impressing God.

Our anxieties might make us more susceptible to this bad faking—we want so much to fit in and be accepted that we grasp for other people's favor. But God's approval is the goal. Keep doing good. . .He will notice.

119
ENVY KILLS

Don't worry about the wicked or
envy those who do wrong.
PSALM 37:1 NLT

Why are sporting events such a big deal? Because human nature is competitive. We want to be (or to support) winners. We long to do better than others physically, mentally, and financially.

While ambition isn't necessarily bad, it can get out of hand. When we cast envious eyes on other people's success, we have a problem. When we are jealous of bad people, we *really* have trouble.

It's so easy to fear we're missing out or falling behind. We're tempted to cheat or lie or steal to keep up. We might think of doing immoral things to fit in.

God says, "Don't!" Don't make wicked people your example. Don't desire what the evil have and do. God has far better things for you, and He will bless you as you pursue them.

Be on the lookout for envy in your life. . .and as soon as you see it, give it to God.

120

MISPLACED TRUST

Some people store up treasures in their homes here on earth. This is a shortsighted practice—don't undertake it. Moths and rust will eat up any treasure you may store here. Thieves may break into your homes and steal your precious trinkets.

MATTHEW 6:19 VOICE

Money creates anxiety for many people. Or more accurately, a lack of money—though even that's a relative thing. A very average economic status in the West would stun people living in poverty in many other countries.

Sometimes we view money as our savior. Not that we think it can buy eternal life, but we see a healthy bank account as vital to our happiness. We want the clothes, electronics, and kind of car that show we've "made it" in this world.

But Jesus reminds us that none of those things last. The phone becomes obsolete. The car gets rusty. The clothes wear out. Your money may be stolen. . .or dwindle due to inflation.

Don't put faith in any physical things. Save your trust for God alone.

121
GUARDIAN ANGELS

For He will rescue you from the snares set by your enemies who entrap you and from deadly plagues.

PSALM 91:3 VOICE

The Bible version called The Voice sometimes drops in a little commentary to help explain a passage. . .and points out that Psalm 91 is one of a handful of places in scripture that hint at "guardian angels." Verse 11 reads, "He will command His heavenly messengers to guard you, to keep you safe in every way."

God has the knowledge and the power to rescue you from any and every situation. There may be times when He chooses to use angels to accomplish that mission. It's possible that they will be the powerful, white-robed creatures that shocked and awed people in Bible times. Or they might be seemingly average people you encounter "unawares" (Hebrews 13:2 KJV).

Whatever the case, know that God always has you covered. He can bring any and every power in the universe to your aid.

122
VISUALIZE THIS. . .

Like a bird protecting its young, God will cover you with His feathers, will protect you under His great wings; His faithfulness will form a shield around you, a rock-solid wall to protect you.

PSALM 91:4 VOICE

Sometimes the Bible gives us an incredible visual to help explain an idea. The Lord as our shepherd (Psalm 23) is one example. The imagery of Psalm 91 is another.

Whether or not you've actually seen a protective mother bird shielding its young from danger, it's something you can readily imagine. And that's exactly how God says He takes care of His own.

Whatever dangers and troubles come our way, God is there to surround us with His "great wings." Think about this: If He fills the whole universe (which He does), His wings are certainly big enough to surround us. And if He was the power behind the whole universe (which is absolutely true), then nothing could possibly overcome His protection.

Why be anxious when our God is so great?

123

PROTECTED FROM DANGER

A thousand may fall on your left, ten thousand may die on your right, but these horrors won't come near you. Only your eyes will witness the punishment that awaits the evil, but you will not suffer because of it.

PSALM 91:7–8 VOICE

The craziness of our world can be frightening. Whether through crime, terror, war, or natural disasters, people get hurt—even killed—every day.

Does Psalm 91:7–8 guarantee that you'll never be affected by such circumstances? No. Many Christians have died in wars and natural disasters, as well as by persecution. We even have a biblical record of the latter.

The promise to us as believers is that we'll avoid "the punishment that awaits the evil." Everyone will die, but Christians are guaranteed a welcome to heaven. The "horrors" that follow the death of the wicked will not touch you in any way. You're kept safe from the ultimate danger—and God will often protect you from difficulties in this world too.

124

IF. . .

If you make the LORD your refuge, if you make the Most High your shelter, no evil will conquer you; no plague will come near your home.

PSALM 91:9–10 NLT

We human beings certainly can't save ourselves. But once we've accepted God's gift of salvation by believing in Jesus, we become responsible for choices that either help or harm our relationship with the Lord.

Notice the conditions in the verses above. If you want to be protected from evil, if you desire to keep the plague away from your home, you need to do certain things. What things? "Make the LORD your refuge" and "make the Most High your shelter."

These are not physical actions, since God is a spirit. Making Him your refuge and shelter is an activity of your spirit, along with your mind. You have to tell yourself—even out loud—that God alone is your hope, strength, and protection. Consciously dismiss any thoughts of your own wisdom, ability, or resources saving you.

125

EVEN WHEN YOU MESS UP. . .

Instantly Jesus reached out His hand and caught and held him, saying to him, O you of little faith, why did you doubt?

MATTHEW 14:31 AMPC

Ever fear that your failures will keep God from loving you? That's not the way He works.

The apostle Peter was inconsistent. He was bold for Jesus. . .until he wasn't. We all know Peter wimped out at crunch time, saying he didn't even know Jesus, who was then on trial for His life. But the Son of God (who *is* God) forgave and restored Peter (John 21:15–19).

That was a huge incident in Peter's life. Today's scripture is part of a smaller, yet still instructive, situation. As Jesus broke the laws of nature by walking on water, good old Peter asked to join Him. At Jesus' invitation, Peter walked on water too—until the wind and waves distracted him and he plunged downward.

Jesus saved Peter, as He'll also do for us. . .even when we mess up.

126

BE HONEST WITH GOD

Lord, my longings are sitting in plain sight, my groans an old story to you. My heart's about to break; I'm a burned-out case.

PSALM 38:9–10 MSG

God can handle your honest emotions. You don't have to approach Him with carefully prepared words. You're welcome to pour out your deepest hopes and fears to Him, even if all you can do is groan. Since He knows everything, God can interpret every muddled thought you bring before His throne. The important thing is that you go!

Sometimes we think our problems bother God. We don't want to bore Him with our troubles. We figure He must have more important things to attend to. But nothing could be further from the truth.

Whatever troubles you is His greatest concern. And the sooner you get honest with Him, the sooner He'll move to help you out.

Tell God when your heart's about to break, when you're feeling burned out. Don't add to your stress by going it alone.

127

THE KEY TO RESCUE

The Lord *says, "I will rescue those who love me.*
I will protect those who trust in my name."
Psalm 91:14 NLT

In one sense, God's love is universal, meaning it's for all people. Every human being is made in His image, and He provides good things—like the sun and rain—for both the evil and the good (Matthew 5:45). And certainly, "God so greatly loved and dearly prized the world that He [even] gave up His only begotten (unique) Son, so that whoever believes in (trusts in, clings to, relies on) Him shall not perish (come to destruction, be lost) but have eternal (everlasting) life" (John 3:16 AMPC).

But the Lord has a deeper, more intimate and long-lasting love for those who follow Jesus by faith. Just like we do, God responds most favorably to those who love and trust Him. These are the people He promises to protect.

The key to receiving God's rescue is relying on Him completely.

128
GUILT AND ANXIETY, PART 1

My guilt overwhelms me—
it is a burden too heavy to bear.
PSALM 38:4 NLT

Sin is a convincing liar. It tells us we'll be happy, free, and fulfilled if we do wrong. Then when we give in to our evil desires, we find we're none of the above. What we are is guilty.

Guilt is "a burden too heavy to bear." We drag through our days worried that others will learn the terrible thing we did—or we're mortified by the fact that they already know. Our anxiety meter climbs into the red as we dread the ongoing fallout of our foolish choice.

But there is a solution, which you'll find in Psalm 38:18 (NLT): "I confess my sins; I am deeply sorry for what I have done."

When you go to God and humbly admit how wrong you were, He responds by applying Jesus' perfection to your life. God basically says, "Jesus took your punishment. You're clean and free. Now go and sin no more."

129
GUILT AND ANXIETY, PART 2

You know what I long for, Lord;
you hear my every sigh.
PSALM 38:9 NLT

Psalm 38, a "psalm of David," bombards us with grief and pain. The author laments his "foolish sins" (verse 5 NLT) and begs God not to rebuke him in anger or discipline him in rage (verse 1). David sounds like he's stressed over something really big, like his adultery with Bathsheba and the arranged killing of her husband, Uriah (2 Samuel 11).

But our sins don't have to rise to that level (or perhaps we should say, "*fall* to that level") to create guilt and anxiety in our lives. And then we cry and sigh to God, saying, "You know what I long for"—release from the mental and emotional pressure we feel.

We've already seen that humble confession is the key that unlocks God's forgiveness and our freedom. When you're feeling guilt over some foolish sin you've committed, never let fear keep you from approaching God for forgiveness.

130
GUILT AND ANXIETY, PART 3

Do not leave me alone, O Lord!
O my God, do not be far from me!
Hurry to help me, O Lord, Who saves me!
PSALM 38:21–22 NLV

Christian guys today enjoy a big advantage over Old Testament "stars" like David: We have God's Spirit living inside us. After Jesus died on the cross for sins and returned to heaven, He fulfilled a promise He'd made by sending the Spirit to live inside all who follow Him by faith.

What some call the "indwelling presence" of God explains why Jesus could say, "I am with you always, even to the end of the world" (Matthew 28:20 NLV). The three-in-one God—Father, Son, and Spirit—lives in believers permanently.

Even when we sin, we don't have to fear that God will leave us. He'll never decide He wants to go far away. Yes, we should deal with our sin immediately to restore our fellowship with Him. . .but God will never ever discard His own.

131
GUILT AND ANXIETY, PART 4

My heart beats fast. My strength leaves me.
Even the light of my eyes has gone from me.
My loved ones and my friends stay away from me
because of my sickness. My family stands far away.
Psalm 38:10–11 NLV

Let's take one more glance at Psalm 38, where David admits that his sins have really messed him up. Though he doesn't say exactly what he did wrong, the guilt from his failure has brought massive anxiety into David's life.

Can you relate to a racing heartbeat? To an overall feeling of weakness? To an internal darkness that even dims your eyes? These aren't always the result of a guilty conscience, but a guilty conscience sure doesn't help such feelings.

Here's the good news: God doesn't expect you to wallow in your guilt. He doesn't want you to live with anxiety. If sin has caused your stress, confess it to God right now. And whatever the cause, talk to Him about your anxiety. He cares.

132
DULLING THE FEAR

"But be on your guard. Don't let the sharp edge of your expectation get dulled by parties and drinking and shopping."
LUKE 21:34 MSG

Once in a while, we find something that moderates the pain of our anxiety. Some people who hate being alone with their thoughts seek out parties—the noisy action helps them to forget their fears, at least for a while. Others turn to drugs and alcohol, which pose obvious dangers. Still others like to buy stuff—the rush of acquiring new clothes or electronics or other physical things helps them to leave their fears behind for a time.

Jesus spoke the words of Luke 21:34, urging His disciples to stay sharp and be ready for His second coming. But the warning can also apply to other areas of life. Beware of the bad trade, swapping anxiety for things that are just as negative, if not worse.

Instead, how about taking a walk, reading your Bible, or praying to your heavenly Father?

133

THE GOLDEN RULE

Make a clean break with all cutting, backbiting, profane talk. Be gentle with one another, sensitive. Forgive one another as quickly and thoroughly as God in Christ forgave you.

EPHESIANS 4:31–32 MSG

For whatever reason, you wrestle with anxiety. It's scary, frustrating, and exhausting. You sure don't want other people to point at you and laugh.

So don't ever do that to anyone else. Make it your aim to follow the apostle Paul's teaching in Ephesians 4:31–32.

That's a lot like Jesus' Golden Rule: "Ask yourself what you want people to do for you, then grab the initiative and do it for *them*." He finished His thought by saying, "Add up God's Law and Prophets and this is what you get" (Matthew 7:12 MSG).

Just imagine how anxieties would melt away if everyone lived up to the Golden Rule. Unfortunately, that won't happen on this side of heaven. But there's nothing that says you can't do your part here and now.

134
TELLING GOD WHAT TO DO

For I am waiting for you, O LORD.
You must answer for me, O Lord my God.
PSALM 38:15 NLT

Normally it's unwise to try to boss around an authority figure. If you tell a teacher, a police officer, or the president what to do, you're probably not going to accomplish much, other than getting yourself in trouble. This is especially true when you're making demands of the ultimate authority, God.

Unless. . .you're repeating His own promises back to Him. When the psalm writer David told God, "You must answer for me," he was basically saying, "You have chosen me for an important job. You have given me responsibility and the promise of Your presence. You can see and hear the attacks against me. Now protect me as I know only You can!"

When you find a promise in God's Word—of peace or hope or joy—say it back to God. Tell Him what to do, respectfully, and expect Him to come through.

135

"AS FAR AS IT DEPENDS ON YOU"

If possible, as far as it depends on you, live at peace with everyone. Beloved, never avenge yourselves, but leave the way open for [God's] wrath; for it is written, Vengeance is Mine, I will repay (requite), says the Lord.

ROMANS 12:18–19 AMPC

Program this scripture into your memory bank—it'll save you a lot of anxiety throughout your life.

Leave all vengeance to God. He has the knowledge and power to effectively repay all your enemies. Your fuming and scheming will only make you miserable—more miserable.

Instead of picking fights, live at peace with everyone. But. . .don't overlook that introductory phrase: "As far as it depends on you." Sometimes you won't be able to live in peace, because other people are—dare we say it?—awful. Just get out of their way. Pray that they'll humble themselves before Jesus and get their lives on track. But don't add to your anxiety by taking responsibility for their bad behavior.

136

GET YOUR REST

In peace I will both lie down and sleep, for You, Lord, alone make me dwell in safety and confident trust.

PSALM 4:8 AMPC

Anxiety is a thief, stealing our peace, our joy, our rest. But God knows you need downtime to recharge your body and spirit. What can you do when fear causes your heart to race, makes your body tense, and keeps your eyes open through the night?

Prayer is certainly appropriate when you can't sleep. But here's something to try even before that: breathe. Sit up or stand, and take a deep breath. Hold it for a while before exhaling. Do this several times to help calm your body and clear your mind. Then you can pray. And then, by God's grace, you might lie down and sleep in peace.

Rest is important to both your physical and mental health. But you often have to calm your nerves before you can enjoy the benefits of sleep. God made oxygen to help.

137

DO WHAT IS RIGHT

Walk away from the evil things in the world—
just leave them behind, and do what is right,
and always seek peace and pursue it.
1 PETER 3:11 VOICE

Let's be very clear: Anxiety doesn't always arise from sin in our lives. But sin in our lives will ultimately create anxiety.

We should obey God out of love and respect for Him. All that we are and have comes from Him, so our good behavior is a way of honoring our Lord.

But doing right is also good for us. When we "walk away from the evil things in the world," when we "do what is right, and always seek peace and pursue it," we are helping ourselves.

Getting and staying on God's path leads us to a happier, healthier place in life. That's not to say that all anxiety will disappear—but it does mean that we'll be better able to handle whatever stresses come our way.

138

DIVIDED LOYALTY

No one can serve two masters. If you try, you will wind up loving the first master and hating the second, or vice versa. People try to serve both God and money—but you can't. You must choose one or the other.

MATTHEW 6:24 VOICE

Jesus demands wholehearted commitment. Matthew 6:24 indicates this truth, as does His comment to people who said they'd serve Him, but wanted to do other things first: "If your hand is on the plow but your eyes are looking backward, then you're not fit for the kingdom of God" (Luke 9:62 VOICE).

As we discussed earlier, our choices and behaviors should all be directed toward honoring our holy God. But doing right also brings good to us. That good can include a lessening of stress and anxiety.

The Bible says that "divided loyalty. . .leaves you dizzy and confused" (James 1:8 VOICE). Who wants to live like that—off balance, wondering, wandering? Focus on Jesus to improve your mental health.

139

PEACE WITH GOD

Now that we have been made right with God by putting our trust in Him, we have peace with Him. It is because of what our Lord Jesus Christ did for us.

ROMANS 5:1 NLV

Anxiety may seem like a mountain in our lives, but it's only a pebble compared to our real problem—the sin that separates us from God.

Remember, not every anxious moment arises from a specific sin in your life. But sin in general—the human rebellion against God that brought a curse on the whole earth—creates the anxieties we feel. In a perfect world, there would be no stress or fear.

That's why Romans 5:1 is such incredibly good news. When we follow Jesus by faith, we are "made right with God." Our own sins are washed away, and we have peace with the Lord. Not peace with the world, which is still broken by sin—but peace with the great Creator who will soon re-create the world in eternal perfection.

140
WHAT DO YOU LOVE?

Those who love Your Law have great peace, and nothing will cause them to be hurt in their spirit.

PSALM 119:165 NLV

In the deepest pit of anxiety, it's hard to find joy in anything. But what do you love when the anxiety has faded into the background for a while? Video games? Sports? Food, cars, getting outside?

God "richly and ceaselessly provides us with everything for [our] enjoyment" (1 Timothy 6:17 AMPC). So, if used properly, any and all of those things can contribute to our pleasure in life.

But to love God's Word—His Law, as Psalm 119:165 calls it—will bring us "great peace." Other pleasures come and go, but knowing scripture deeply (and by that, knowing the Author of scripture deeply) provides personal benefits that excel all others. . .and last forever.

That's because God's Word is "living and powerful" (Hebrews 4:12 NLV). It's exactly what we need to defeat the dead weakness of anxiety.

141
BROUGHT INTO HARMONY

When we worship the right way, God doesn't stir us up into confusion; he brings us into harmony.
1 CORINTHIANS 14:33 MSG

This passage explains how Christians should "worship the right way." But it also makes an important point about life in general: God wants human beings to live in harmony.

He desires believers of different backgrounds to love each other and live in peace together. But God also wants peace and harmony *within* each follower of Jesus. As Romans 5:1 (AMPC) says, "Since we are justified (acquitted, declared righteous, and given a right standing with God) through faith, let us [grasp the fact that we] have [the peace of reconciliation to hold and to enjoy] peace with God through our Lord Jesus Christ."

God doesn't want us stirred up and confused. He "is not a God of confusion and disorder but of peace and order" (1 Corinthians 14:33 AMPC).

Go ahead—ask Him to bring your mind and emotions into harmony.

142
DON'T FIGHT

The seed that flowers into righteousness will always be planted in peace by those who embrace peace.

James 3:18 voice

When you're frustrated and fearful, it's easy to be short and rude with other people. But we must never allow our anxiety to become an excuse for bad behavior.

God wants peace between Himself and people, and among all human beings. That peace unfolds when people humble themselves before Jesus, who serves as the mediator between God and humanity (1 Timothy 2:5). Sadly, not everyone will follow Jesus, so this peace is limited at the present time. But righteous people "embrace peace" since that is God's desire.

Our anxious feelings must never erupt into angry words or actions toward others. That will hurt people we care about. It may cause people who need to know Jesus to turn away from Him. And it certainly won't do anything to reduce our anxiety.

So don't fight. Consciously plant the seeds that flower into righteousness by embracing peace.

143

YOU HAVE RESPONSIBILITIES

So be careful how you live; be mindful of your steps. Don't run around like idiots as the rest of the world does. Instead, walk as the wise!

EPHESIANS 5:15 VOICE

Without question, anxiety is tough. It darkens our thoughts, weakens our bodies, and dampens our hope. But as we've already noted, we must never allow anxiety to become an excuse for poor behavior.

The Bible consistently teaches two things: First, salvation is a gift received by faith. Second, we are responsible for making good choices with the wisdom and power God provides.

That's the key: God provides all the good we need. For His own wise reasons—which are far beyond our understanding—He allows some people to struggle with anxiety. But He also offers Himself, His Word, and His strength to help us through.

Now help yourself. Commit to your responsibilities—living carefully, being mindful of your steps, walking in wisdom. Of course you'll need help. . .so ask the Lord to provide.

144
DON'T GO IT ALONE

Get all the advice and instruction you can,
so you will be wise the rest of your life.
PROVERBS 19:20 NLT

Do you ever consider how God answers prayer? For a Christian guy facing a financial crisis, God could just cause cash to materialize in his wallet—but it's much more likely that the Lord will prompt a fellow believer to step in and share his resources. For a guy facing anxiety, God could just cure you the moment you cry out to Him. But He may choose to send wise and sensitive fellow believers into your life to share support, encouragement, and their hard-won experience.

In your battle with fear, don't go it alone. Human struggles are nothing to be ashamed of, and you won't impress God with your solitary efforts. When someone speaks up offering help, hear them out. And if they aren't showing up, seek them out. As Proverbs says, "Get all the advice and instruction you can."

145
DON'T MAKE THINGS WORSE

Fools think their own way is right,
but the wise listen to others.
PROVERBS 12:15 NLT

Not every piece of advice is good or helpful. But "there is safety in having many advisers" (Proverbs 11:14 NLT). When you need guidance, seek it out from a lot of people—especially older ones who follow Jesus consistently. Then weigh everything you hear, comparing it to what the Bible says about the issue. And before making any final decision, be sure you pray for God's perspective.

Anxiety messes with our minds, so let's be sure we never let it lead us into folly. Even if it seems scary to reach out for advice, do it anyway. You have it on God's authority that "fools think their own way is right." You also have God's thumbs-up for listening to others.

Don't ever make things worse by disregarding the wisdom good people can bring to your life.

146
GETTING BEAT UP?

Take my side, God—I'm getting kicked around, stomped on every day. Not a day goes by but somebody beats me up; they make it their duty to beat me up.

PSALM 56:1–2 MSG

Ever felt like this psalm writer? Like you're just getting whomped on? Maybe other people don't understand your anxiety, and they're making fun of you—or maybe they're actually trying to help but saying all the wrong things. Or perhaps the kicking and stomping and beating up arises from inside yourself. One of the worst aspects of anxiety is the self-recrimination.

Notice what the psalmist did first: He called out to God. Perhaps it sounds simplistic, but everything we do should start with Him. He may tell you to stop and breathe for a minute, revisit a passage in His Word, or deal with a conflict with someone else. If you go to God immediately and then do what He says, things will get better as He works in and through your life.

147
PRAISE WINS

When I get really afraid I come to you in trust. I'm proud to praise God; fearless now, I trust in God. What can mere mortals do?

Psalm 56:3–4 msg

Perhaps you noticed this. . .but if not, the scripture above immediately follows the verses from the previous reading. They were kind of a downer, recounting how beat up the psalm writer, David, felt.

But then, when he was "really afraid," David turned to God in trust. He'd seen God protect him and bring him through all kinds of challenges—the dangers of bears and lions when he was a young shepherd, the danger of the Philistine warrior Goliath, and the danger of his own king, Saul, whose jealousy toward David turned murderous.

Because God had already treated David so well, he could proudly praise his Lord. . .and that changed everything. Praise made David "fearless" as he realized that God was bigger and stronger than anything else. What could any created thing really do to hurt him?

148

SEEING GOD. . .

I have seen you in your sanctuary and gazed upon your power and glory.
PSALM 63:2 NLT

We are physical beings in a physical world. We are limited in knowledge, strength, and time. We are deeply affected by the curse of sin. All these truths contribute to anxiety.

God is not limited by anything. As a spirit, He fills the entire universe. His knowledge, power, and existence are infinite. He is the very definition of good, untouched (and untouchable) by sin.

When we begin to grasp these truths—and realize how much He loves us—our anxieties diminish. If we can "gaze upon" God's power and glory and make ourselves believe that He'll use every bit of His goodness on our behalf, what is there to fear?

How can you see God in His sanctuary? This vision starts with His written Word, which tells you everything He saw fit to share about Himself. Dig deeply. When you see God, all other things fall into place.

149

MAKING SURE YOUR PRAYERS ARE HEARD

If. . .My people (who are known by My name) humbly pray, follow My commandments, and abandon any actions or thoughts that might lead to further sinning, then I shall hear their prayers from My house in heaven, I shall forgive their sins, and I shall save their land from the disasters.

2 CHRONICLES 7:13–14 VOICE

God made this promise to King Solomon, saying He would hear His people's prayers on three conditions: First, they needed to pray humbly—God would not listen to prideful prayers. (That's kind of a funny phrase when you think about it.) Second, they needed to follow God's commands—like any of us, He's more inclined to do things for people who treat Him respectfully. Third, they needed to "abandon" their sinful inclinations—to walk away from their evil desires and not return to them.

These conditions applied to the entire nation of Israel under Solomon's rule. But they certainly applied to the Israelites individually. . .and still make sense for us today.

150

THE LORD IS FOR YOU

The L*ORD is for me, so I will have no fear. What can mere people do to me? Yes, the* L*ORD is for me; he will help me. I will look in triumph at those who hate me.*

PSALM 118:6–7 NLT

This truth should banish all fear from your life: The Lord is for you. The one true God, the creator and sustainer of all things, commits Himself to everyone who follows Jesus by faith. What could any mere person—or any mere circumstance—do to harm you?

This truth *should* banish our fear. . .but all of us are broken people living in a broken world. We may still feel anxiety and fear even though we can consciously acknowledge the truth we read in God's Word. But fighting our fear begins with our mental acceptance of these truths—God is awesome, He is for us, and He will help us.

Tell yourself these truths over and over again and ask God to bring your emotions along.

151
VINDICATED BY GOD

But no instrument forged against you will be allowed to hurt you, and no voice raised to condemn you will successfully prosecute you. It's that simple; this is how it will be for the servants of the Eternal; I will vindicate them.

ISAIAH 54:17 VOICE

Let's focus on the last four words of this verse: "I will vindicate them." What exactly does that mean?

You get a hint from the preceding sentence: God says that He will protect you—His own son by adoption—from any "instrument forged against you," from any "voice raised to condemn you." This shows one meaning of the word *vindicate*—namely, to defend.

But the term can also mean to free from allegation or blame. And to vindicate is to justify—to regard as righteous and worthy of salvation. If all that isn't enough, *vindicate* even has an older meaning of setting free and delivering.

How much anxiety does God's vindication cover? When He's on your side, what is there to fear?

152
DON'T STAY AWAY

Return to the Lord your God, for He is full of loving-kindness and loving-pity. He is slow to anger, full of love, and ready to keep His punishment from you.

JOEL 2:13 NLV

Avoiding God is a major cause of stress in a Christian's life.

We stay away for all kinds of reasons. Perhaps we've committed a sin and we're afraid God is angry with us. Maybe we just generally don't feel worthy of Him. Sometimes we resent Him for the difficult things He's allowed in our lives. Or it might be any of a thousand other reasons.

But none of them are good, right, or helpful reasons. God is our devoted Father, "full of loving-kindness and loving-pity." He's not quick to get angry, like we so often are. . .and He's "ready to keep His punishment from you." In other words, we don't ever need to fear God's response if we simply go to Him in humble faith.

Don't ever stay away—return to the Lord your God.

153
ONLY JESUS

When they looked up, Moses and Elijah were gone, and they saw only Jesus.
MATTHEW 17:8 NLT

Moses and Elijah were Old Testament VIPs. . .so when they appeared with Jesus at His transfiguration, Peter, James, and John were impressed. Always the talker, Peter babbled about setting up memorial shelters, but the voice of God the Father quickly ended that: "This is my dearly loved Son, who brings me great joy. Listen to him" (Matthew 17:5 NLT). The disciples fell to the ground in terror, but Jesus gently pulled them back up, saying, "Don't be afraid" (verse 7 NLT). Raising their eyes, Peter, James, and John saw "only Jesus."

We are impressed by many people—hopefully our parents, maybe a teacher or coach, possibly a politician or business leader or athlete, perhaps that amazing girl in English class. But no one is as impressive as Jesus. Nobody can say "Don't be afraid" with the power He has to back it up.

In your battle with anxiety, always remember: "Only Jesus."

154
HOW MANY ENEMIES DO YOU HAVE?

No longer will I fear my tens of thousands of enemies who have surrounded me!

PSALM 3:6 VOICE

We all have enemies of some sort. They may be people who truly hate us for some reason, or they may be the mental and emotional bugaboos that inhabit our minds and spirits. But would you say you have "tens of thousands of enemies"?

King David did. Psalm 3 was written as he ran for his life from his crazy good-looking son Absalom. The ambitious young man who had already murdered a half brother now set his sights on David's throne. Absalom had turned on the charm to make himself "the favorite of the people of Israel" (2 Samuel 15:6 VOICE). He gathered an army of followers bent on dethroning David.

Yet the king—God's chosen one—could speak the words above because "the Eternal supports me" (Psalm 3:5 VOICE).

Guess what? The same God supports you too.

155
LIKE AN EAGLE

When your soul is famished and withering,
He fills you with good and beautiful things,
satisfying you as long as you live. He makes you
strong like an eagle, restoring your youth.
PSALM 103:5 VOICE

As a teen guy, you're considered a youth. But when you feel anxious, your age by itself doesn't confer strength. So even if this promise of "restoring your youth" doesn't thrill you, the idea of God making you "strong like an eagle" should.

We definitely understand a "famished and withering" soul. Anxiety dries us up and leaves us weak. But God has an infinite supply of "good and beautiful things" to give us. He's pleased to satisfy our souls with goodness—His goodness, His own life.

When will He do that? As we pull our eyes off ourselves and start to praise Him: "O my soul, come, praise the Eternal with all that is in me—body, emotions, mind, and will—every part of who I am—praise His holy name" (Psalm 103:1 VOICE).

156

RELAX, GOD LOVES YOU

The Lord is full of loving-pity and kindness.
He is slow to anger and has much loving-kindness.
He will not always keep after us.
PSALM 103:8–9 NLV

Back in the day, you'd find the message "Smile, God Loves You" on bumper stickers, T-shirts, buttons, and jewelry. Today, for those of us who wrestle with anxiety, let's adapt that phrase to say, "*Relax*, God loves you."

Psalm 103 reminds us that God is very patient—He's "slow to anger." God is compassionate—He's "full of loving-pity and kindness." God doesn't choose to hammer us over our failures—He "will not always keep after us."

This doesn't mean we can live any way we choose. But if we genuinely want to follow God by faith in Jesus Christ—however imperfectly we do so—we become part of God's family, both now and forever. As His adopted sons, we can count on His patient, generous, and everlasting love. This Father-son relationship will see you through every imaginable challenge.

Relax, God loves you!

157

YOUR SINS ARE GONE

He has taken our sins from us as far as the east is from the west.
PSALM 103:12 NLV

At base level, sin causes anxiety. There are times when a particular sin we've committed weighs on our hearts and causes stress. But generally speaking, it's the sin we're all born into that creates fear and anxiety, because it separates us from our loving Creator. He is "the God of all peace" (Romans 15:33 VOICE), and He wants to share peace with us. How? By removing our sin.

In Old Testament times, people offered animal sacrifices for sin. But those sacrifices only covered sin—they didn't remove it. And they were temporary, since the next sin required a new offering.

We have the benefit of living in the New Testament era, after Jesus became the perfect, once-for-all sacrifice for every sin. When we believe this truth, our sin isn't just covered—it's completely paid for and removed.

When your sins are gone, anxiety loses its previous power.

158
GIVE ME A BREAK!

He knows what we are made of.
He remembers that we are dust.
PSALM 103:14 NLV

Have you ever had a really demanding teacher or coach (or maybe a parent), and you just wanted to shout, "Give me a break!"? You thought, *Hey, I'm still a teenager. I'm still figuring things out. Can't you see that I'm not yet at your level?*

God understands. He recognizes that you are, literally, a blob of dust. That's not an insult but an objective fact—the first man was created out of the dust of the earth, and we follow in his dirty footsteps. When we die, we return to the dust that makes up our bodies.

Because we are such weak, unimpressive creatures, God goes easy on us. He shows us incredible love and mercy by offering His free salvation through Jesus Christ. When we receive this gift, God makes us His much-loved sons. And even when we fail, He's eager to forgive as soon as we confess.

159
GOD MADE YOU

Bless God, all creatures, wherever you are—
everything and everyone made by God.
Psalm 103:22 msg

Here's an important reminder: God created everything. . .including you.

Think of the pride you take in whatever you've made. Whether you built a sturdy wooden bookcase, wrote a compelling short story, or assembled a lightning-fast gaming system, you feel good about what you've done. And you're not going to let anyone steal, damage, or even belittle your work. You want to protect what is yours.

God feels much the same way. His world is a beautiful place, the care of which He delegated to the one creature He made in His own image—human beings. Even though we people and our world are marred by sin, God still takes great pleasure in His work. And He's especially proud of His children, everyone who chooses to follow Jesus Christ by humble faith.

Try looking at your anxieties through the lens of God's incredible love for you. Then bless Him, wherever you are.

160
WHEN GOD SAYS NO. . .

Each time he said, "My grace is all you need. My power works best in weakness." So now I am glad to boast about my weaknesses, so that the power of Christ can work through me.

2 CORINTHIANS 12:9 NLT

God's wisdom and power can accomplish anything. He could easily cure our every anxiety with a single word. But sometimes—often, actually—He says no to our prayers. That easy fix from Him doesn't show up in our lives.

We don't always like God's ways. But if He's God (and He is), we have to believe that He knows best. And somehow, the anxiety He allows in our lives must have purpose.

According to the apostle Paul in 2 Corinthians 12, that purpose is for us to experience and understand God's grace. Our weaknesses force us to reach out for His strength. And in His strength, we become strong.

Keep praying, asking for what you want. But until God says yes, trust Him to see you through.

161
LIVE WITH PURPOSE

So watch your step. Use your head. Make the most of every chance you get. These are desperate times!
EPHESIANS 5:15–16 MSG

Stay busy with good, useful things. That might help to keep your anxiety at bay.

What kind of things? Personal Bible study. Serious prayer. Service to widows and orphans and the church of Christ. Charitable deeds in your community.

Don't be busy for the sake of busyness, but apply yourself to things that have a truly eternal value. When you're honoring God—by knowing Him better and making Him known to others—your anxieties and fears will have less space to fill in your mind. You may even find that you're really fulfilled when you "make the most of every chance you get."

Your feelings may not change right away—as you know very well, fear can be a sticky thing. But if you consciously step up to live with purpose, you might begin to sense that anxiety is losing its grip on your spirit.

162

JEREMIAH'S EXAMPLE

"I called out your name, O God, called from the bottom of the pit. You listened when I called out, 'Don't shut your ears! Get me out of here! Save me!' You came close when I called out. You said, 'It's going to be all right.'"

Lamentations 3:55–57 MSG

They call Jeremiah "the Weeping Prophet" for his emotional reaction to the Babylonian destruction of Jerusalem. "Rivers of tears pour from my eyes at the smashup of my dear people," he wrote elsewhere in Lamentations (3:48 MSG). Even the name of the book means "an expression of sorrow or mourning."

The death and devastation in Jerusalem were appalling, and they obviously unsettled Jeremiah. And yet right in the middle of his dreary, depressing book of Lamentations, the weeping prophet could dry his eyes long enough to look up to God. Jeremiah could swallow hard and cry out to God for help—and hear the Lord say, "It's going to be all right."

Let's try to follow Jeremiah's example.

163
THERE IS ALWAYS HOPE

At once Jesus spoke to them and said, "Take hope. It is I. Do not be afraid!"
MATTHEW 14:27 NLV

Without looking up Matthew 14, do you know the story this verse comes from? If you said, "Jesus walking on the water," pat yourself on the back.

Can you feel the anxiety of the disciples caught in a crazy storm on the Sea of Galilee? Waves are slamming their boat, and Jesus—who just miraculously fed five thousand men with one boy's lunch—isn't with them. They're thinking, *We're doomed!*

But with Jesus, there is always hope. In this case, He made His way to the disciples, casually walking up and down on those raging waves. Then He called out, "Take hope. It is I. Do not be afraid!"

When the storm rages around you, when you fear your boat is about to sink, Jesus is there. And what He said to the Twelve He says to you now: "Take hope. It is I. Do not be afraid!"

164
DELIGHT AND REJOICING

"The LORD your God is living among you. He is a mighty savior. He will take delight in you with gladness. With his love, he will calm all your fears. He will rejoice over you with joyful songs."

ZEPHANIAH 3:17 NLT

Would it help you to know that God takes pleasure in you? And not just a little—He delights and rejoices over you. In fact, you bring a song to God's lips!

When you're struggling with anxiety or fear or frustration or any other difficult, negative emotion, stop and tell yourself this: *The God of the entire universe made me. He knows me. He is glad and joyful at the very thought of me!*

Sometimes we forget how very personal God is. Yes, He's vast—infinite, actually. But He also knows every individual human being, whom He made in His own image. And He's especially high on those of us who have accepted His offer of salvation. He actually delights and rejoices over us. . .over *you*.

165

NO FEAR OF BAD NEWS

They do not fear bad news; they confidently trust the LORD to care for them.

PSALM 112:7 NLT

Not afraid of bad news? That sounds great! But who are "they" in this verse?

Look earlier in Psalm 112 to see that "they" are people who "fear the LORD and delight in obeying his commands" (verse 1 NLT). "They" are also "generous, compassionate, and righteous" (verse 4 NLT). "They" sound a lot like people who follow Jesus' teaching on the greatest commandments—to love God and then love other people (Matthew 22:37–39).

So here is the challenge for us: If we want to leave our anxieties behind, if we'd like to live without fear of bad news, we should pursue God wholeheartedly and reach out in love to people around us.

Is this always easy? No. But it's definitely worth any effort we put into the pursuit. And don't forget that when you step out in faith, God is always there to give you strength.

166
ENEMIES DEFEATED

Their hearts are confident, and they are fearless, for they expect to see their enemies defeated.

PSALM 112:8 VOICE

Not every enemy is human. Certainly many are, whether it's a guy at school who enjoys hassling you or it's a wild-eyed terrorist who hates everything about you, your faith, and your nation. But enemies come in all forms—including sickness, death, and fear. But one day, every enemy will be defeated by the God who promises a perfect eternity.

Your heart can be confident in this because your all-powerful God has the ability to make it happen. Some of your human enemies will ultimately join your side. . .but those who refuse God's kindness will be put in their rightful place. Every other enemy will fade into a forgotten past as God makes all things new (Revelation 21:5).

Knowing that the people and things that stress you now will someday trouble you no longer, do you think you could be fearless? Or could you at least fear less?

167
IN EVERY DETAIL

David continued to address Solomon: "Take charge! Take heart! Don't be anxious or get discouraged. God, my God, is with you in this; he won't walk off and leave you in the lurch. He's at your side until every last detail is completed for conducting the worship of God."

1 Chronicles 28:20 MSG

God is with you in every detail of your life. Nothing that's important to you is ever unimportant to Him. He is constantly aware of your thoughts and actions, and He's pulling for you to get them right. In fact, He's eager to provide the wisdom and strength you need to do just that.

The aged King David shared these truths with his son and successor Solomon. The young man was preparing to lead Israel politically—but he also had responsibility for the nation's spiritual well-being. And David assured Solomon that God would always be there to help him.

As a follower of God through faith in Jesus, you have this promise too.

168

WHEN, NOT IF

When you go forth to battle against your enemies and see horses and chariots and an army greater than your own, do not be afraid of them, for the Lord your God, Who brought you out of the land of Egypt, is with you.

DEUTERONOMY 20:1 AMPC

Details are important, especially when we read the Bible. If we're not paying close attention, we might end up believing things that aren't true.

Some people think that after they accept Christ, their lives will suddenly become happy and easy. Jesus does bring a lasting joy to our hearts, and He's always ready to help us—but these benefits often get us *through* hard times, not *out* of them.

Notice in today's scripture that Moses said "when" you're outnumbered in battle, not "if." Tough times will happen, so be sure you're not thinking otherwise. But even when hardships come, "do not be afraid of them." The Lord your God is with you.

That's another "when," not "if."

169

PRAY FOR PROTECTION

God's angel sets up a circle of protection around us while we pray.

Psalm 34:7 msg

Feelings of vulnerability lead to anxiety. If you're by yourself at night in a bad part of town. . .if you're just not understanding calculus. . .if there's a weird sensation in some part of your body—you might envision all kinds of bad outcomes. You could have a terrible disease, you could flunk out of school, you could be robbed, beaten, and killed. . .

Chances are, those worst-case scenarios will never happen. But the fear itself is real, and it is something you'll need to address. The best way is through prayer.

When you take your anxieties to God, you acknowledge that He's there, He's bigger than your problems, and He's able and willing to help. And the verse above adds another important reason to pray: God will send His angel to set up "a circle of protection" around you.

Don't miss the important timing—this protection happens *while* you pray. So pray a lot.

170
CONFIDENT, NOT AFRAID

When evil people come to devour me, when my enemies and foes attack me, they will stumble and fall. Though a mighty army surrounds me, my heart will not be afraid. Even if I am attacked, I will remain confident.

PSALM 27:2–3 NLT

The context of a scripture is important. Basically, that's the "neighborhood" of a passage—the details of what surrounds the verse or verses you're reading.

What's the context of Psalm 27:2–3? What made David confident and fearless even when he was surrounded by "a mighty army" that wanted to "devour" him?

Verse 1 shows that he viewed the Lord as his "light" and "salvation," as his protective "fortress." And in verse 4, he expressed his great joy in God: "The one thing I ask of the LORD—the thing I seek most—is to live in the house of the LORD all the days of my life, delighting in the LORD's perfections" (NLT).

Fear fades in the light of this kind of passion for God.

171

TEACHABLE

Teach me Your way, O Lord. Lead me in a straight path, because of those who fight against me.

PSALM 27:11 NLV

Are you teachable? Are you willing to take advice from older, wiser people in your life? Can you admit that you don't know everything, that others might have some knowledge that you could use?

Thinking you've got everything figured out—or knowing you don't but trying to convince people you do—is a bad way to live. You'll create unnecessary stress and anxiety in your life by being unteachable.

But seeking out wisdom from other people, and especially from God, will inevitably help you. God knows everything, so asking Him for wisdom (James 1:5) is a slam dunk. And your parents, aunts and uncles and grandparents, teachers and coaches and pastors have all experienced a lot of life, gaining wisdom that could help you to avoid some crazy, stressful situations if you're willing to listen and learn.

Always be teachable. You'll please God and help yourself.

172
PATIENCE AND HOPE

I would have been without hope if I had not believed that I would see the loving-kindness of the Lord in the land of the living. Wait for the Lord. Be strong. Let your heart be strong. Yes, wait for the Lord.

PSALM 27:13–14 NLV

Kids—and we'll include teenagers in this category—get a bad rap for impatience. There's truth in that, but there are also very few adults who have mastered the art of waiting. Whatever their age, Christians are called to patience, as the Bible is packed with commands to "wait."

Many times, the word *wait* is followed by "on the Lord." He has His own timetable, which is often quite different from our own. But because He is the all-knowing and all-powerful God, His timing is always best.

We'll relieve anxiety and stress in our lives as we learn to wait on God, as we convince our own impatient spirit that He has everything under perfect control. And as we grow in patience, we gain hope.

173

ANXIETY OVER EVIL PEOPLE

How long will they speak with arrogance?
How long will these evil people boast?
They crush your people, LORD, hurting
those you claim as your own.
PSALM 94:4–5 NLT

Do you get stressed when you see oppression in the world? Do hatred and wars between nations make you feel anxious? Do bullies at school or in the neighborhood trouble you, even when you're not their target?

It's perfectly natural to hate the arrogance of evil people who hurt others. And it's okay to raise your concerns to God; the men He picked to write down His Word often questioned such things.

But never forget that God knows exactly what's going on. He knows exactly who's causing trouble. God cares, just like you do—to an even greater extent—and He will make things right.

If you want some serious encouragement on the topic, put this book down for a bit and read all of Psalm 94. Your anxiety over evil people will one day be completely forgotten.

174

SOLID GROUND

Jesus the Anointed One is always the same: yesterday, today, and forever.
HEBREWS 13:8 VOICE

Change is stressful. Attending a new school, moving to a different city, losing a grandparent, or dealing with sickness can cause all kinds of anxiety. Those are major life issues, but even smaller changes can feel overwhelming. The truth is that a sea of change swirls around each one of us every day.

So a verse like Hebrews 13:8 is incredibly powerful. In a world that's constantly spinning, literally and figuratively, Jesus is our solid ground. He does not change. The love that sent Him to the cross two thousand years ago is the same love He feels for you today. The power with which He healed the sick and raised the dead in the first century is the same power He wields in the twenty-first.

Perfection cannot change, or else it wasn't perfection to begin with. Jesus was, is, and always will be perfect. He is your solid ground.

175

THE RIGHT TIME

For everything that happens in life—there is a season, a right time for everything under heaven.

ECCLESIASTES 3:1 VOICE

You might think, *Why am I battling anxiety right now? I want to enjoy my teen years, but I have this dark cloud over my head. . .*

The verse above provides an answer, even if it's tough to accept: God has a particular time and reason for everything that happens in our lives. Much of what He sends is good, even very good. Some of what He allows in our lives is tough. . .even seemingly impossible.

Whatever the case, God is in every moment of every hour of every day, celebrating with us, commiserating with us, providing the strength we need to get through the hard times.

And within God's plan, hard times are never wasted. He uses them to draw us closer to Himself, which is really the purpose of this life. Then He encourages us to pass along the comfort He gives us (2 Corinthians 1:4).

176
HEALTHY LIFE CHANGE

Do not act like the sinful people of the world. Let God change your life. First of all, let Him give you a new mind. Then you will know what God wants you to do. And the things you do will be good and pleasing and perfect.

ROMANS 12:2 NLV

If you want to break down the Christian life to its most basic parts, Romans 12:2 is a good starting point. We must let God change our hearts, and we do that by accepting Christ—by believing in Jesus' death on the cross as payment for our sins. We allow Him to give us a "new mind," the "mind of Christ" (1 Corinthians 2:16 NLT). Then we can know what God wants, and our thoughts and actions can be "good and pleasing and perfect." When we're part of God's family by faith in Christ, letting Him lead us by His Spirit, we won't "act like the sinful people of the world."

This is healthy life change.

177

SLOW AND STEADY GROWTH

This is the reason we do not give up.
Our human body is wearing out. But our
spirits are getting stronger every day.
2 CORINTHIANS 4:16 NLV

Maybe this seems like a verse for old people. . .when you're young, you don't really think of your body as "wearing out." On the other hand, can you say your spirit is "getting stronger every day"?

When we're anxious, it's especially tough to sense the growth and strengthening of our spirit. But if you truly follow God by faith in Jesus, if you genuinely want to honor Him by your life, you'll become "stronger every day." You'll be like a tree that gets bigger and more resilient over time. You can't judge that day by day, but year by year and decade by decade, yes—the growth becomes obvious.

Earlier in this book, we considered Jeremiah 17:7–8, a passage that (like Psalm 1:1–3) compares our Christian life to a healthy tree. Why not revisit those verses for a little guidance and encouragement?

178
THE BIGGER PICTURE

The little troubles we suffer now for a short time are making us ready for the great things God is going to give us forever. We do not look at the things that can be seen. We look at the things that cannot be seen. The things that can be seen will come to an end. But the things that cannot be seen will last forever.

2 CORINTHIANS 4:17–18 NLV

Your anxieties probably don't seem like "little troubles. . .for a short time." When you're dealing with persistent fear, you feel like you're up against the Rock of Gibraltar—it's huge, unyielding, permanent.

But compared to eternity, everything on earth is simply a blip. God has prepared "great things" for the perfect forever that Christians anticipate. Your job in the here and now is to stay faithful to God as He makes you ready for that incredible future.

This is the bigger picture that you currently "see" by faith. But someday, and soon, your faith will be sight.

179
KEEP LEARNING

Wise men and women are always learning,
always listening for fresh insights.
PROVERBS 18:15 MSG

Wisdom has no age limit. You can be wise at nine or ninety-nine. . .a range that certainly includes you. Make sure you're one of the "wise guys"—in the most positive sense of the phrase—by committing yourself to continual learning.

The most important learning is spiritual. Listen for fresh insights on how to know, love, and serve God. You'll get this wisdom from older, more mature believers who've proven their Christian faith over time. Ask them to share what they've learned, and then ask God to help you put into practice anything that applies to you personally.

This will be a huge help in dealing with your stress and anxiety. Many people have struggled with them but found their way through by God's grace.

So keep learning from faithful teachers. Then, as you feel like your own life is making sense, be sure to share your wisdom with others who need it.

180

WHERE YOUR VICTORY BEGINS

Every part of Scripture is God-breathed and useful one way or another—showing us truth, exposing our rebellion, correcting our mistakes, training us to live God's way. Through the Word we are put together and shaped up for the tasks God has for us.

2 TIMOTHY 3:16–17 MSG

So we arrive at the end of our journey together—the final entry in our review of 180 Bible verses for conquering anxiety. We've considered 179 passages so far. The 180th is simply a reminder of the power and value of God's Word.

The Bible is actually breathed out by God. Its pages don't just contain truth—they *are* the truth. Scripture provides us with everything God knew we would need for life. So we are wise to spend as much time and energy as we possibly can studying the Bible.

In your battle with anxiety, God's Word—being "alive and powerful" (Hebrews 4:12 NLT)—is where your victory begins. May God grant you His success as you persevere!

SCRIPTURE INDEX

OLD TESTAMENT

Proverbs

Ecclesiastes

Isaiah